Theology for a nuclear age

Theology
for a nuclear age

Gordon D. Kaufman

Manchester University Press

The Westminster Press

Copyright © 1985 Gordon D. Kaufman
Published by Manchester University Press
Oxford Road, Manchester M13 9PL, UK
and The Westminster Press
Philadelphia, Pennsylvania 19107, USA

British Library Cataloguing in Publication Data
Kaufman, Gordon D.
    Theology for a nuclear age:
    1. Atomic warfare—Religious aspects—
    Christianity
    I. Title
    230   BR115.A85

    ISBN 0-7190-1766-1
    ISBN 0-7190-1793-9

Library of Congress Cataloging in Publication Data

Kaufman, Gordon D.
    Theology for a nuclear age.

    Includes bibliographical references and index.
    1. Theology, Doctrinal—Addresses, essays, lectures.
    2. Nuclear warfare—Religious aspects—Christianity—
    Addresses, essays, lectures. I. Title.
    BT80.K38 1985   230   84-25803
    ISBN 0-664-21400-2
    ISBN 0-664-24628-1 (pbk.)

Filmset in Great Britain
by Pen to Print
Colne, Lancashire
Printed in United States of America

2   4   6   8   9   7   5   3   1

Contents

Preface

When Professor A.O. Dyson of Manchester University wrote to me inquiring if I would be willing to give the Ferguson Lectures for 1984, I welcomed the invitation, because it seemed to me an excellent opportunity to work out more fully some ideas which had been stirring in my mind for some time and which I thought should be presented to a wider public. In my presidential address to the American Academy of Religion in 1982, on 'Nuclear eschatology and the study of religion',[1] I had suggested to my colleagues that the nuclear age into which humankind has now moved – an age in which it is possible we may utterly destroy not only civilisation but humanity itself – challenges scholars in theology and in the study of religion to do some radical re-thinking about our disciplines and about some of the presuppositions taken for granted in our work. But I was unable in that context to spell out to any great extent what I had in mind. The invitation to give the Ferguson Lectures presented an excellent opportunity to sketch out more fully the sort of reconception and reconstruction which it seemed to me was needed in Christian theology, so I happily accepted it and prepared the set of lectures now being published in this book. I hope that scholars in other fields of religion studies will undertake to think through in a similar way what their disciplines might contribute to a better understanding of the momentous crisis now facing humankind, as well as the way in which this crisis demands and opens up new ways of thinking about their scholarly work and its methods.

This book bears the somewhat presumptuous title, *Theology for a Nuclear Age*. That correctly characterises its intention, but it greatly overstates its achievement. In a small volume like this it would not be possible to take up all the theological issues raised by the new age into which access to nuclear power has brought humankind; many important questions that should be dealt with are not mentioned at all, and the issues to which most attention has been given may seem to some quite restricted in scope. Even such an important theological topic, for example as the significance and task of the church as the bearer of Christian symbols and traditions, has been left completely undiscussed. In spite of these limitations there is, however, a justification for the title. This book focuses directly and forthrightly on issues which must be at the heart of any theology which seeks to address the nuclear question seriously: (1) What does the nuclear age mean for humanity's basic self-understanding, and thus for our conception of theology as a human activity? (2) In light of these matters, how are we to interpret the two central symbols in terms of which Christian faith orients and understands itself – *God* and *Christ*? Since answers to questions as fundamental as these will decisively shape a whole theology, one can properly claim, I think, that what is presented here is the kernel, at least, of a theology for a nuclear age.

The first chapter argues that with the advent of the nuclear age and the power to bring all human life to an end, humankind has moved into a radically new religious situation, one completely unanticipated in the Christian tradition (or, for that matter, in any of the other great religious traditions); in consequence, if Christian faith is to provide adequate orientation in today's world, it will be necessary to re-examine axioms and claims hitherto seldom questioned by Christian theologians, reconstructing them in quite radical ways. With this task in view I present, in the second chapter, a conception of theology as an activity of 'imaginative construction' (rather than simply interpretation of tradition), arguing that such a view frees the theologian to undertake the kind of radical criticism and reconstruction of traditional concepts and attitudes that our unprecedented situation demands. The third and fourth chapters, then, turn directly to the two central symbols of Christian faith, *God* and *Christ*, attempting to show that, when thoroughly deconstructed and properly reconceived, they significantly illuminate our contemporary historical crisis and suggest sorts of action appropriate for addressing it. Thus, the four chapters seek to present the nuclear age as raising extremely serious issues for Christian theology, and they also sketch a way for theology and faith to respond to this challenge.

To some it might seem a bit odd to take up these issues now, nearly forty years after the first atomic bombs were dropped. Have theologians just recently become aware that the new age into which we have moved has important implications for Christian reflection?

Though a few writers apparently realised immediately that Christian self-understanding must change drastically if it is to come to terms with the new religious situation,[2] most theology done in the last thirty years reflects very little sensitivity to this question. Humankind has managed to avoid nuclear war during this period, despite many international crises, and this apparently has lulled most theologians (along with many others) into a certain complacency about the significance of the atomic age for their work; the fact that we had moved into a totally unprecedented historical and religious situation went largely unrecognised and was little discussed. In the last few years, however, as Europeans and Americans have come to realise that the steady development and stockpiling of nuclear weaponry has created a veritable Doomsday Machine in our midst, and that we now in fact have the capacity to wipe humankind off the face of the earth – and there is a good possibility that we may do just that – a second period of reflection on the significance of the nuclear age has begun. To some of us it has become clear that a much more radical probing of the theological significance of the unprecedented new powers and responsibilities which have recently fallen to humans must be undertaken. The present book is intended as a contribution to this conversation which is now getting underway.

I want to make it clear that I do not regard this small book as a conclusive argument for my point of view but rather as presenting a kind of *picture* – a way of *seeing* Christian faith and Christian theology today; and I am inviting my readers to look carefully at this picture to see whether it does not throw light on certain important issues which have been obscured by earlier views. I am asking readers to consider whether the new situation in which humanity now finds itself – in which we are able, by the mere press of a button, to destroy our entire world as well as humankind itself – isn't in a significant way 'out of sync' with the central traditional claim about God's sovereignty over the world. The notion of God's sovereignty seems to have become fundamentally irrelevant to understanding what we should do in the new situation in which we find ourselves – it is unclear how it can bear on our problems one way or the other – and yet belief in the divine sovereignty was at the very heart of traditional faith. Thus a significant tension – a logical tension – is set up between our intuition or feeling that humankind has moved into a thoroughly new and radically unique situation and the traditional claims about the meaning and importance of trusting ourselves fully to the love and care of God. In these chapters I have tried to articulate just what this tension is and whence it has come, and I have proposed a reconception of God and of Jesus Christ – and

ix

thus of Christian faith and salvation – which I think addresses and dissolves it.

No one is compelled, of course, to accept the picture I have painted here. It is quite possible to continue to assert the traditional claims about God's providential care and power, even in the face of the present nuclear crisis; and many Christians apparently wish to do just that. But this can be done only at the cost of denying that the situation in which we today find ourselves is radically new and unprecedented. The logical tension between the traditional view of God's sovereignty and the destructive power which appears now to rest unequivocally in human hands forces us to go one way or the other with our thinking: we can take our sense of living in a truly new situation, one not anticipated in our religious traditions, as a valid and important insight which must guide our further religious reflection and our ways of living and acting in the world – and then many traditional Christian claims, and much else of traditional Christian faith, will need drastic reconstruction; or we can hold on to the fundaments of traditional faith and deny that our contemporary situation is as novel as it might initially appear to be. I have become persuaded that the former alternative is the correct one, and that is the picture I have tried to present in these lectures. Others, of course, will conclude that the latter view should be maintained. I hope, in any case, that this little book will help readers to focus seriously on this question and will encourage them to think through their own position on it.

I trust that this book will not leave anyone with the impression that the technological reordering of human life – and the nuclear crisis which is its most dramatic symbol – is the only important question to which theology must address itself today. As the 'liberation theologies' have emphasised, widespread poverty and hunger in the world, issues of social justice, racial, religious and gender discrimination and many other forms of dehumanisation all raise extremely serious questions for theology and for the way in which theology is done. In this book, taking the nuclear crisis as my pre-eminent example, I have argued that radically new theological thinking is now a necessity; but it would be just as disastrous for theology as for politics to focus all efforts on a 'single issue'. New imaginative construction is needed across the whole range of human experience and problems, and only as that comprehensive work is accomplished will we begin to discern what Christian theology can and should be in today's world.

I make no claims, therefore, to having presented here the only sort of interpretation of God and Christ and salvation which is viable or relevant today; doubtless there are other perspectives, other ways of reconstructing the central Christian symbols, which have much to offer. I hope that those who see such other ways of illuminating our deepest contemporary problems will share them with us all, for Christian theological work must always be an on-going conversation among many voices.

There are many who have contributed to making this book possible; only a few can be acknowledged here. I am especially grateful to the Faculty of Theology of the University of Manchester in England for inviting me to give the Ferguson Lectures in 1984, thus providing the occasion for putting together these reflections on 'theology for a nuclear age'; the hospitality and many kindnesses accorded me while I was in Manchester will be long remembered. The first two lectures include material based on articles originally published in the *Journal of the American Academy of Religion*;[3] I am grateful to the *Journal* for giving permission to use that material here. Unless otherwise indicated, all biblical quotations have been taken from the Revised Standard Version of the Bible, copyrighted 1946 and 1952 by the Division of Christian Education of the National Council of Churches of Christ in the USA, and are used by permission. Finally, it gives me particular pleasure to acknowledge how much this book owes to the numbers of women students over the years who have refused to allow me to rest content with traditional patriarchal and authoritarian patterns of theological reflection and have helped me move toward the more ecological and open sort of theologising which (I trust) is to be found in these pages; it is to the criticism and the constructive suggestions of my students that I have always been most indebted in my thinking and writing.

G.D.K.
Cambridge, Massuchesetts
30 May 1984

Notes

[1]Since published in the *Journal of the American Academy of Religion* (March 1983) 51:3–14.
[2]For some examples, see note 3, chap. 1, below.
[3]'Nuclear eschatology and the study of religion', *op. cit.*; and 'Theology as imaginative construction', *JAAR* (1982) 50:73–9.

I

Nuclear eschatology

Some months ago I had the privilege of visiting the city of Hiroshima in Japan, the first city in history to be devastated by a nuclear explosion. As everyone knows, I am sure, there is a lovely Peace Park in Hiroshima, located near what is believed to have been the centre of the explosion. The layout of the park is simple and unpretentious. Within the park are to be found a number of beautiful sculptures memorialising the terrible event that took place there, and also the skeletal remains of one building left partially standing after the explosion. There are two museums where photographs and documentary movies can be viewed, as well as a large model of the city of Hiroshima showing how fully it was devastated; a number of rocks and other sorts of remains show in various ways the consequences of the blast and the heat. The collections in the museums are not large because, of course, the devastation was so complete that there was very little left to collect. One item that I found particularly moving was a portion of a stone stairway which had been in front of a bank some distance from the explosion's centre. Apparently someone had been sitting on those steps at the moment of the blast, because a distinct shadow of a human form could be seen in one spot where something had absorbed much of the heat of the explosion, thus protecting that part of the rock from undergoing the transformation which the enormous heat worked on it elsewhere.

Surrounding the Peace Park is the bustling modern city of Hiroshima, now completely rebuilt and showing no outward signs of the awful event that happened there nearly forty years ago. The park itself, though certainly a place where one must reflect on our human capacity for destruction and cruelty, also has the effect of uplifting one's spirit by its simple austere beauty and, not least, by the happy faces of the little children among the endless stream of visitors, evoking a sense of new life and hope for the future. So, overall perhaps, it is the sense of resurrection and the human ability to overcome tragedy, and not the destructiveness and finality of death, that is the lasting impression with which Hiroshima now leaves the visitor. That is as it should be, because the bomb that fell on Hiroshima did not, in fact, mean a final end for that community. Though much was destroyed and there was – and still is – enormous suffering, and though many were killed, the life of the people has been rebuilt; and the horrible desolation now remains largely in the form of living memories and a memorial park. Thus, even that awful demolition and death has been transformed into meaning and beauty, into creativity and new life. Precisely in being remembered, the bombing of Hiroshima has become for all of us an important symbol – doubtless a symbol of horror and evil and of what must be prevented from ever happening again – but, for just that reason, an exceedingly meaningful moment in the life of humanity. Hiroshima has been resurrected from horrible desolation into creativity and new life for all women and men everywhere.

Hiroshima, of course, is not unique in this respect. Through its powers of memory and memorial the human spirit is often able to transcend the most horrible evils it has experienced, transforming them into moments of symbolic meaning which illuminate our common human condition. So it has been with Buchenwald and the other Nazi death camps; so also with the massacre of Armenians by Turks decades ago and of American Indians by European settlers taking over the North American continent; so also with the assassination or execution of persons who have offered profound leadership and spiritual insight to their people, a Gandhi, a Martin Luther King, a Socrates – above all, at least to Christians for whom his crucifixion became the very centre of a redemptive faith, Jesus Christ. The deeper the human tragedy, so it seems, the greater the power of the human spirit to work redemption in the lives of those who remember and cherish it.

In this respect Hiroshima can easily be a very misleading symbol for us. For it stands not only for what happened once – or twice – almost forty years ago, but also for what may be coming this year or the next: an all-out nuclear war. And that event, if it happens – unlike Hiroshima, and unlike all the other tragedies which humans have brought upon each other – may not be remembered and memorialised, thus acquiring new and redemptive meaning. For it is quite possible that after a generation there will be no one left to remember it. The potential nuclear holocaust which we confront must signify for us the possible extinction of humanity, an absolutely unique event in human history which can have no redemptive significance for us humans. We must not allow the resurrection of a Hiroshima, or other resurrections either, to lull us into a failure to recognise the utter uniqueness, and the full horror, of the tragedy we in the late twentieth century confront. It is an event which no generation before 1945 had even been able to imagine.

To many this may seem like an obvious overstatement – or even an outright untruth – since the end of human history has long been contemplated in the religious traditions of humankind as well as in modern scientific speculations about the evolution of the cosmos and about entropy. Western religious traditions, for example, have been informed by the expectation of a final judgement by God in which the wheat will be separated from the chaff and all that is in opposition to God's purposes will be destroyed in a fiery holocaust as God brings those purposes to their ultimate consummation. The historicist world-view – which developed in ancient Israel, was appropriated and universalised by the Christian movement, and eventually became decisive in shaping the modern western mind – easily lent itself to a strong consciousness of futurity, and thus it was a natural matrix for the emergence of ideas of a temporal end to the world. Though some always hoped that the consummation of history would be beneficient and healing of humanity's ills – at least for the faithful – others, like the prophet Amos, seemingly saw nothing but utter desruction in the final future. Jesus' preaching, as is well known, was informed throughout by the expectation of an imminent catastrophic ending of history, and there have been many Christian movements in the past two thousand years which picked up this strong eschatological consciousness, and looked forward to the return of the Lord on the clouds of heaven virtually momentarily. Thus the idea of a catastrophic end to history is 'old stuff' for western religous and cultural traditions, though it is a notion that has been largely suppressed, perhaps, in intellectual circles of the West since the Enlightenment.

However, in the religious eschatology of the West the end of history is pictured quite differently than we today must face it. For it is undergirded by faith in an active creator and governor of history, one who from the beginning was working out purposes which were certain to be realised as history moved to its consummation. The end of history, therefore – whether viewed as ultimate catastrophe or ultimate salvation – was to be God's climactic act. A consummation of this sort was something that the faithful could live with – even

3

look forward to with hope – for it would be the moment when God's final triumph over all evil powers was accomplished.

In contrast, the end of history which we in the late twentieth century must contemplate – an end brought about by nuclear holocaust – must be conceived primarily not as God's doing but as ours. Moreover, it is difficult to think of it as part of a grand plan bringing about the salvation of humanity; it is, rather, the extinction – the total obliteration – of human life on earth. Not only the ending of all our individual hopes and aspirations – a finality which each of us individually must face as we contemplate our own deaths – but an ending of all hopes and all aspirations, indeed, of all hopers and aspirers, of all future generations who could carry on the quests and projects, the values and meanings, the institutions and ways of life in which humankind has invested so much over many thousands of years. Beyond the total human destruction which such a conflict might well bring, the poisoning and radical transformation of the earth's upper atmosphere together with the advent of a so-called nuclear winter could make impossible the survival of most forms of life, thus returning our planet to its original largely barren and dead condition – except for one important difference: the atmosphere of those primordial ages here on earth was conducive to the evolution of countless species of life; the atmosphere after a nuclear holocaust would be irredeemably poisoned for a very long future.

In his recent book, *The Fate of the Earth*,[1] Jonathan Schell catalogs the almost unimaginable destruction and suffering which a nuclear conflict would bring, possibly culminating in the total extinction of humanity. Then he goes on to point out how important it is to make a clear distinction between the suffering and deaths of billions of persons, on the one hand, and the further almost ungraspable issue of the obliteration of the entire human future, on the other.

> The possibility that the living can stop the future generations from entering into life compels us to ask basic new questions about our existence, the most sweeping of which is what these unborn ones . . . mean to us. No one has ever thought to ask this question before our time, because no generation before ours has ever held the life and death of the species in its hands . . . how are we to comprehend the life or death of the infinite number of possible people who do not yet exist at all? How are we, who are a part of human life, to step back from life and see it whole, in order to assess the meaning of its disappearance? . . . Death cuts off life; extinction cuts off birth. Death dispatches into the nothingness after life each person who has been born; extinction in one stroke locks up in the nothingness before life all the people who have not yet been born. . . . The threat of the loss of birth . . . assails everything that people hold in

4

common, for it is the ability of our species to produce new generations which assures the continuation of the world in which all our common enterprises occur and have their meaning.[2]

It is striking that it was a secular writer who most dramatically called public attention to this new historical situation in which humanity finds itself. Most religious folk, however seriously they have concerned themselves with the nuclear crisis, seem not to have paid much attention to what is perhaps its most significant religious feature: the momentous *change* in the human religious situation brought about by the possibility that we humans, by ourselves, will utterly destroy not only ourselves but our species, all future generations, thus bringing the entire human project, through which and for which many hundreds of generations have labored, to an abrupt and final halt.[3] Though some occurrences in recent history – such as the Nazi holocaust or the Cambodian massacres, or earlier, the attempted obliteration of American Indian cultures – certainly demonstrate vividly the human capacity for massive evil, they barely foreshadow the kind of finality we are here trying to contemplate. Why have so few theologians and other religious folk (other than apocalyptic fundamentalists) not been examining, from their special point of view, this momentous religious fact right before our eyes? Why have they not sought to understand the contemporary religious situation through it, and sought to interpret the uniqueness of this potential calamity in terms of the modes of understanding and insight made available to us by our religious traditions? I would like in these lectures to point out some of the implications which our new religious situation has for Christian faith and thought and to suggest some reasons why much Christian theology has not come to terms with it very successfully.

An important point of Jonathan Schell's is that our new-found ability to obliterate, and thus the possibility that we will obliterate, all future human life, is so novel and strange that it is difficult for us to grasp what we are up against. It is difficult enough – some philosophers have held it impossible – to imagine our own individual deaths; in terms of what concepts or images, then, is the death of the entire human race, the end of all human projects and hopes, to be brought before the mind? The idea is so abstract, so empty of meaning, that we can scarcely grasp what we are talking about.

Here again, it is important that we contrast our situation today with the eschatological visions found in many religious communities from ancient Israel to the present: in most cases there was an expectation that a faithful remnant would survive the catastrophe and, indeed, be glorified; in even the bleakest visions of that dark day, there was the satisfaction that God's righteous will would at last prevail and that God's glory and honor would be vindicated. So for traditional eschatology there was always some positive meaning – some humanly significant meaning – in the consummating events of history. But our situation is different. The potential catastrophe that we are here called upon to contemplate is empty of any such meaning. We are left with our imaginings of the earth becoming a barren desert, devoid of life like the moon above us, and with an atmosphere filled with poisonous gases. The only thing human about this event is that we men and women will be the ones who have done it, we will be responsible for having brought on the catastrophe; when it happens, nothing human, nothing humanly significant whatsoever, will remain. How are we to think such an utterly abstract notion, a notion of an earth from which the human has been totally and irrevocably removed? And how are we to take such an idea seriously? It is hardly surprising that most people don't.

Not only is the annihilation of humanity itself almost unthinkable by us; the procedures by which we ordinarily assess alternative courses of action – by appeal to values and standards and norms important to us – also fail to apply in any clear way to this new situation. Schell makes the point in this way.

> . . . none of [our standards] have any meaning or application unless one first assumes the existence of . . . mankind. Anyone who prizes the usefulness of things assumes the existence of human beings to whom things can be useful; anyone who loves justice assumes the existence of a society whose parts can be brought into relationships that are just; anyone who loves beauty and truth assumes the existence of minds to which the beautiful and the true can manifest themselves; anyone who loves goodness assumes the existence of creatures who are capable of exhibiting it and being nourished by it; and anyone who wishes to promote the common good assumes the existence of a community whose divergent aims it can harmonize. These standards of worth, and any others that one might think of, are useful only in relating things that are in life to one another, and are inadequate as measures of life itself.[4]

Admittedly, Schell's argument is stated in overly anthropocentric terms, but his central point is valid nonetheless. We are in an unprecedented situation, facing a possible calamity the consequences of which we can scarcely conceive and the dimensions of which we have no adequate means of evaluating, a calamity, nonetheless, of which we human beings would be the sole agents, a catastrophe for which we would be exclusively responsible.

Although this event would obliterate most of what gives our lives meaning, the act of bringing it on is heavy with meaning – and it is all negative. There is no redeeming value, so far as I can see, in any of the human intentions and actions that bring this event about.

The possibly imminent annihilation of humanity – brought about by our own hands – brings us up against the ultimate limits of our human existence. I am not competent to survey the many religious traditions of humankind to see what they might offer in the interpretation of this event; but I would like to examine briefly certain western, largely Christian notions, to see how they might bear on the problem before us as well as to see how this problem might bear on them.

Of all the world religions, few have emphasised human creativity and responsibilities as have those traditions grounded in the Bible. Yet not even western religious traditions have contemplated human powers and responsibilities of anything like the scope and magnitude which we must consider here: humankind was never believed to have the power utterly to destroy itself; that power lay with God alone. If we wish to interpret our catastrophic event in terms of these traditions, two alternatives appear open to us. Either we can assert that the ultimate catastrophe, if it comes, is in some significant sense God's will and God's doing, that the annihilation of humanity which God had contemplated during the time of Noah is now coming to pass through a nuclear holocaust instead of a flood. Or we may hold that God, as the redeemer and saviour of humankind as well as our creator, has so bound Godself to humanity and the human enterprise – in the covenant made with us in Jesus Christ, as Karl Barth would say – that this utterly calamitous self-destruction of humanity will never be allowed to occur. Each of these alternatives affirms the ultimate sovereignty of God over the events of history – an indispensable point for biblical faith. This provides a ground for human hope in face of this potential catastrophe, and it implies that the proper human action here – as always – is to be conceived in terms of obedience to the divine will. But in focusing this way on God's activity, both of these interpretations obscure what is central and novel in this potential event as it confronts us today, namely, that it will be we human beings who are absolutely and fully responsible if this catastrophe occurs, that this event confronts us primarily as an act of human doing rather than of divine will, and that both our actions and our hopes with respect to it, therefore, must be directed toward the transformation of our human institutions and policies.

7

Some fundamentalists on the far religious right, following out the implications of the biblical apocalyptic imagery of an earthly holocaust as the ultimate expression of God's sovereignty over history, are apparently willing to go so far as to suggest that a nuclear disaster, if it ever comes, could only be an expression of the purposes of God; hence, any who work to prevent such a climax to human history are in fact guilty of opposing God's will.[5] Along with such convictions, as one might expect, goes the demand that the western nations arm themselves to the teeth in preparation for the coming Armageddon. But surely to take such a position is an ultimate evasion of our responsibility as human beings in this whole matter; indeed, it is demonically to invoke the divine will as a justification for that very evasion.

The other direction one can go with traditional theological interpretation, holding that God's providential care will not allow us to destroy ourselves in a nuclear holocaust, does not push us toward this sort of demonic extreme; but it too has the effect of cutting the nerve of human responsibility with its assurance that, however horrible a nuclear war might be and however much we are obliged to work against such a calamity, ultimately we can be confident that we humans will not – on our own – be able to bring human history to its end.

Obviously, nuanced variations and combinations of these theological alternatives can be worked out, and some of these can certainly provide powerful incentives to struggle against a nuclear disaster, as the widespread peace and disarmament work by religious groups shows. But all such interpretations confront a serious problem: they are attempting to grasp our new religious situation – in which *human* power and responsibility confront us as so overwhelming and frightening – in terms of a symbolism of divine sovereignty which really cannot contain or interpret this idea, and which thus helps to conceal the true nature of our predicament rather than illuminate it. When the traditional Christian promise of an afterlife for the faithful is added to this emphasis on the divine omnipotent sovereignty, our human sense of the importance of these earthly events and developments is further weakened.

The stark fact of total human responsibility for the earthly future of humanity, which a potential nuclear catastrophe symbolises, calls into question all this traditional talk – held together so tightly and meaningfully in the symbol of the divine sovereignty – of God's power and purposes and love as the proper and only adequate ground for hope in our desperate situation. This fact demands that we ask much more seriously than many have yet done whether it is

8

not necessary to reconsider some of the most fundamental axioms of western religious symbolism and faith. Humanity's 'coming of age', to use Bonhoeffer's phrase, means that traditional images of divine providential care guaranteeing ultimate human fulfilment have become not only outmoded; they have become misleading and dangerous in certain important respects, and they must be thoroughly reworked. The personalistic conception of God, so powerfully presented by the traditional images of Christian and Jewish piety, seems less and less defensible in face of the issues humanity today confronts – not only the nuclear crisis, but the Nazi holocaust, our ecological problems, the population explosion, the decisions forced upon us by modern biological science. And the anthropocentric, even henotheistic, forms which these faiths have usually taken historically, far from being salvific of the human, now appear to be part of the problem. If radically transformative moves are not, or cannot be, made in these western faiths, these traditions, they will not be capable of grasping and illuminating the full dimensions of the situation with which we must come to terms. In these pages I will suggest certain changes which seem to me required in some of the fundamental Christian conceptions.

The point I am making here, that changes in the historical situation in which we find ourselves – empirical historical changes – themselves call for, indeed force upon us, changes in our religious symbolism and in the frames of reference within which we make our value judgements and moral choices, goes counter to a central assumption of many today. Despite the fact that western religious faiths have understood themselves as created in and through a movement of historical contingencies – what has been called 'salvation history' – adherents to these faiths have, for a very long time, been quite resistant to reconceiving their most fundamental convictions under the impact of new historical developments. Claiming divine revelation as their ultimate authority, most theologians have seen their task to be the presentation of the values and norms, the doctrines and ideas, of the particular tradition to which they subscribe, and the possibility of empirical disconfirmation of central religious claims has been largely ignored or disavowed; some have even argued that in principle it is impossible. Not only in theology, moreover, but in contemporary philosophical reflection as well, descriptive and historical studies and claims have often been sharply distinguished from normative claims and proposals, and it has been held that each of these must be dealt with independently of the other. 'Fact' and 'value', 'is' and 'ought', are logically distinct from and independent of each other, it is said, and it is a category

9

mistake, therefore, to suppose that changes in either of these logical types could, or should, in some significant way affect our thinking about the other. The scientific or historical pursuit of truth – of 'facts' – is, and must be, 'value free'; moral and religious and other value commitments rest, and are to be justified, on grounds independent of existential or factual considerations.

I want to suggest that, in light of the new religious situation in which we find ourselves, these sorts of claims by theologians and philosophers are called into question and superseded. They presuppose that life can properly be lived and knowledge pursued in terms of what is already existent and given, the values and norms and truths carried by some supposedly revelatory or other cultural tradition and the empirical data uncovered by science and history. But the new situation in which we find ourselves shows that it is a mistake to regard our human world as grounded on any fixed and finished givens, whether values or facts. Both fact and value, as the possibility of nuclear catastrophe makes clear, are always very fragile and unstable.

Let us try to focus our attention for a moment on the special way in which the future, the possible, impinges on human life, impinges on the present, thus producing this inescapable fragility.

Futurity, possibility, has always had a very peculiar relationship to the present, to existing empirical realities. But until recently it has not been difficult for us to overlook the full significance of this special connection of future with present, of possibility with actuality. We have been able to limit our concerns in our conception of knowledge, for example, to the present and the past, i.e., to what we called the 'facts' of what is now the case or what has been the case. We felt (with good reason, we thought) that we could take for granted that the future was going to be there, at least for our children if not for ourselves, that it would always keep coming, tomorrow and tomorrow and tomorrow. Thus it was easy to neglect the real importance which futurity has for human living and reflection in every present. This ignoring of the significance of futurity for human life has had its effects. Specifically, with respect to our interests here, it has shaped the self-understanding of theology.

It was taken for granted by many theologians, for example (as by the traditionally religious), that life could and should be lived largely out of the faith-orientations and the values generated in the past and carried now by authoritative traditions. These would provide meaning and guidance sufficient for any contingency that might arise, for any future which human beings might face. No empirical

10

situation would or could disconfirm these; as Paul put it, *nothing* 'can separate us from the love of God in Christ Jesus our Lord' (Rom. 8:38–9). But such a stance simply ignores the real openness and contingency of the future, now so vividly in view before us.

Our human being, even that existential dimension of our being which we call 'faith', always runs out into possibility, into what does *not* exist; it is delimited by the continuous impingement of the future with its openness and unpredictability. People do lose their faith upon occasion; the meaning which life had held for them does sometimes slip away as they fall into despair; they can be, and may well find themselves, separated from 'the love of God in Christ Jesus'. Similar things, of course, must be said about what we take to be knowledge or truth, whether scientific or philosophical or theological. The 'facts' of yesteryear provide material for humorous gibes today; the 'certainties' and 'truths' of today will appear tomorrow, in quite unpredictable ways, as confusions and illusions.

Our theological and philosophical concepts of contingency and finitude are intended to remind us of these matters, that we are living in a world in which much is unexpected and unknown, much is imponderable and ultimately unknowable, a world in which we are not in control. And our religious speech about the ultimate Mystery of human life and its meaning – or meaninglessness – expresses our sense of the unfathomable depth and ultimate darkness of life, a depth and a darkness with which the various human religious symbolisms have always struggled, as they sought to provide orientation and meaning for human communities. The possibility now, that in a nuclear holocaust we may annihilate not only ourselves but all future life on earth, brings us face to face in a new and profound way with this mystery of our common human existence, as it forces us to confront forthrightly the paradox of our finitude and our power, of our knowing and our ultimate un-knowing. Whereas in earlier generations that mystery seemed in a sense something imposed upon us from outside, something rooted in human lack of knowledge, in human weakness, today it is our own enormous knowledge and power which, paradoxically, we do not know how to control or properly use: the mystery and incomprehensibility of life wells up from within us, as it were; our finitude and weakness shows itself most frighteningly to be deeply hidden within our very power and knowledge. The more the future yawns before us as unknown – as fearful possibility, as potential destruction of our way of life, of all we hold dear – the more we are seduced into attempting to seize full control of that future by trying to deter absolutely the enemies threatening us; and so we try to

11

secure our future through multiplying the new power in our hands with ever larger stockpiles of weapons, and, in consequence, we succeed only in moving closer to annihilation. It is our own knowing and doing that seems to be destroying us; how can we possibly come to terms with that?

The fact that we can scarcely imagine what this annihilation could be or what it might mean; that none of the moral and other values and standards, which we customarily use in assessing our situation and the courses of action open to us, seem directly applicable; that our traditional religious symbols and frames of orientation do not quite fit as they were intended and that we of the late twentieth century are thus sprung loose as a generation, facing this horrible contingency naked and alone, opens up for us in a fresh way the starkness of the mystery of human life – a starkness with which religions and theologies have long struggled in the past, but which they have often softened and masked for their devotees.

Our contemporary historical situation demands that we engage these religious and theological questions directly and do so now. There is no avoiding them: we may be about to annihilate all future human life, and we must take responsibility for that fact. We must try to understand it, and we must seek for symbols which can appropriately interpret it. For this is the point in human history where we live, and these are the issues which have been thrust upon us whether we like it or not. There is no possible retreating from these responsibilities of this hour – particularly we who are citizens of the great superpowers who possess atomic weapons. These tasks are central and defining features of our lives as human beings in the so-called civilised world in the late twentieth century; and they bear in a very particular way on those professionally concerned with religion and theology. Just as medical doctors and nuclear scientists have definite professional responsibilities with respect to the crisis confronting us all, so do theologians and philosophers of religion.

It has been the task of each generation of theologians to reinterpret the religious tradition to which they were heir in the light of the new historical situation in which they found themselves. This has often meant, as we shall note in the next chapter, that theologians felt bound to work within the constraints of certain fundamental religious commitments and definitions which they could not violate, and thus theology usually has been an essentially conservative enterprise; but it also implied that a certain creative response to the contemporary historical and cultural situation was always demanded of the theologian, a response that went beyond everything to be found in tradition and involved, thus, the creation of a position or point of view or concept that was in certain respects theologically new. In the next chapter we shall explore in some detail the significance of this dialectic between received tradition and the creation of theological novelty. I bring it up now only to make clear why – if indeed we do confront a radically novel historical situation (as I have contended) – there can be no doubt of the special responsibility this lays on theologians as they proceed with their reflection and their constructive work.

If it is the case that humankind has moved into a historical situation unanticipated either by biblical writers or subsequent theological commentators, a situation of much greater human knowledge, power and responsibility than our religious traditions ever imagined possible, then we – Christian theologians and ordinary Christian believers alike – dare no longer simply assume that we know from authoritative tradition or past revelation the correct values and standards, i.e., the correct faith-orientation, in terms of which life is to be understood and decisions and actions are to be formulated. Theologians may no longer regard themselves largely as handers-on of traditions; they must be prepared to enter into the most radical kind of deconstruction and reconstruction of the traditions they have inherited, including especially the most central and precious symbols of these traditions, *God* and *Jesus Christ*. If theology is truly to help provide meaning and orientation for human life in today's world – its perennial task – it must come fully to terms with the facts of that world, including especially that very peculiar fact-which-is-not-yet-a-reality, the possibility of our annihilating future human existence. As the heteronomy and authoritarianism of tradition in theology are thus overcome, theologians will find themselves becoming open to insights and understandings, points of view and life orientations, symbols and values drawn from the many diverse traditions and cultures of humankind, both secular and religious, scientific and historical as well as theological. If this happens, one may dare to hope, theological reflection will begin once again to provide significant orientation for life even in today's radically new historical situation.

Let me conclude with two brief remarks. First, I trust it is obvious that although I think we confront a situation unique in human history, this does not mean all past insights and knowledge are thereby overthrown, and we now must begin from scratch. Much of what I have said about human existence, about the mystery in which life is ensconced, about finitude and contingency, is of course rooted in traditional religious and philosophical reflection. But in our time those roots are bringing forth a new flower – if it is a flower – namely

13

a new and profounder awareness both of the extent of human power and of the enormous threat of contingency, thus contributing to a new sense of the ultimate mystery at the centre of human life. Though other arguments can be given against the overly heavy dependence of theological reflection on authoritative tradition, I believe the potential calamity facing all of humankind today brings home with a new force the falseness and the abstractness of this style of thinking. Reflection on the meaning of the potential annihilation of humanity can, perhaps, enable us to come to our senses about some of the assumptions we have been making in Christian theology and can help us reorient our thinking in a significant way. And this in turn should make our theology bear more obviously and directly on the crisis confronting us all.

Second, in these remarks I have focused on the significance of the possibility of nuclear holocaust for the reorientation of Christian theology. When one puts the matter that way, it may seem that I have trivialised to an extreme the enormity of the event we are considering: in the face of such a potential catastrophe, who could care about such things as recasting theology? The disproportion is so great as to be comic. I trust no one will suppose that I regard the principal demand made upon us by the threat of nuclear holocaust to be that we reconceive our academic work. It is obvious that political and moral imperatives of the most urgent sort are here laid upon us all. We must work with far greater effectiveness toward stopping the nuclear arms race and, indeed, toward total nuclear disarmament; we must find a way of breaking the back of the system of sovereign nation-states; we must reorient our priorities of consumption and distribution of the world's goods; we must stop poisoning our environment; we must find a way to live with one another productively and justly on this earth, and without warfare among major political units. It is really the possible annihilation of humanity that we must take into account now, and this above all we must each find some way to address if we are to take up our full responsibilities in today's world.

There is no question, I think, that the possibility of nuclear holocaust is the premier issue which our generation must face. If Christian faith is to provide significant guidance in this crisis, the central Christian symbols will need to be reconsidered and reconstructed in important ways. We shall attempt to take some steps in that direction in chapters III and IV; but before we can turn to those issues, it is important to think our way through to an understanding of theology somewhat different from that which has usually been advanced. To that task we will turn in the next chapter.

14

Notes

[1] Jonathan Schell, *The Fate of the Earth* (New York: Avon Books, 1982).

[2] *Ibid.*, pp. 116–18.

[3] There were, it should be noted, some theologians who realised early the religious novelty of the advent of the nuclear age, but their insight seems not to have had much impact on subsequent theological discussion of the issues at stake. Henry Nelson Wieman, for example, could write: 'The bomb that fell on Hiroshima cut history in two like a knife. Before and after are two different worlds. That cut is more abrupt, decisive, and revolutionary than the cut made by the star over Bethlehem . . . it is more swiftly transformative of human existence than anything else that has ever happened. The economic and political order fitted to the age before that parachute fell becomes suicidal in the age coming after. The same breach extends into education and religion.' *The Source of Human Good* (Chicago: University of Chicago Press, 1946), p. 37. And that same year the 'Calhoun Commission', appointed by the Federal Council of Churches of Christ in America to advise the churches, stated that: 'it seems . . . likely that by misdirection of atomic energy, man can bring earthly history to a premature close. His freedom, then, is more decisive and dangerous than we had suspected. In making man a little lower than the angels, God seemingly has laid on him a weight of responsibility that has not only personal but cosmic import.' *Atomic Warfare and Christian Faith* (New York: The Federal Council of the Churches of Christ in America, 1946), p. 20.

[4] Schell, *The Fate of the Earth*, p. 124.

[5] See *The Boston Globe*, 2 May 1982, p. A-1 for a survey of some contemporary opinions of this sort. For a widely read detailed elaboration of such a position, see Hal Lindsey, *The Late, Great Planet Earth* (Grand Rapids, Mich.: Zondervan, 1970).

15

II
Towards the reconception
of theology

The dropping of the atomic bomb on Hiroshima on 6 August, 1945, brought humanity into a radically new historical situation. Techno-logical advances had now placed into human hands new powers of destruction so massive that the accepted conceptions of warfare as an instrument of national political policy were rendered obsolete for the great powers; and humankind entered a period of cautiously feeling its way in international relations, gradually working out the conception of mutual deterrence, according to which the nuclear powers would prevent each other from making war by the threat of overwhelmingly destructive retaliation. Following out this policy of Mutually Assured Destruction (or MAD, as it became so appro-priately called), huge stockpiles of increasingly powerful nuclear weapons have been built up by the several nuclear powers, as the arms race has spiraled out of control. We now have on the ready nuclear explosives which could not only set off the most horrifyingly destructive war humankind has ever seen; it is not unlikely that their massive release would both thoroughly poison the earth and its atmosphere and blot out the sun's light and heat for months, thus making the continuance of human life, and much other life as well, impossible. Humankind has in its own hands the means to obliterate itself.

How should we approach this terrifying new situation theologi-cally? What can Christian theology say to it or about it? Clearly, it is a predicament not envisaged anywhere in the Bible or by subsequent Christian writers up to 1945. Although many Christians have sought to interpret this crisis in terms of traditional concepts and principles, it cannot be taken for granted that they apply; indeed, as I suggested earlier, some of the most fundamental traditional Christian notions, e.g. about the sovereignty and love of God, have become in

16

certain respects dangerously misleading. Does that mean, then, that Christian faith has no way to come to terms with our most serious contemporary dilemma? If we assume that theology is essentially an activity of translation or interpretation in each new present of tradition handed on from the past – and this is the way it has usually been understood – one cannot hope for much new insight to emerge from confrontation with a completely unexpected situation of this sort. At most we might get new versions of old doctrines – as, in fact, has occurred in much Christian reflection on the nuclear crisis, however probing and moving it has been.

But this more or less traditional view of the theological task, I want to argue, is a misleading and mistaken one, resting on certain presuppositions which are no longer tenable. Most prominent among these is the principle of *authority* on which theology has traditionally been based. According to this principle, theological truth is not something we humans discover (or create) in our work; it is, rather, something already present and available in tradition – especially the Bible – awaiting our appropriation. Our task as Christian believers and theologians is to extract the truth from the traditional writings in which it is contained and to discover its meaning for our time and situation. What the truth is, is already determined; we are simply to believe and seek to understand. The task of theology, then, is to work out of tradition and to hand on tradition.

This authoritarian conception was held for a very good reason. It was believed that this tradition, within which and out of which believers and theologians worked, was rooted in God's own revelation to humanity. God spoke in the past through a series of prophets (as reported in the Old Testament) and in Jesus Christ, through whom God came into human history in definitive revelation. In this tradition, therefore, particularly as recorded in the Bible which has often been thought of as the very 'word of God', the truth about God and humanity and Christ is to be found. The truth to be found here is not just ordinary human truth, discoverable by human insights and human methodological reflection and always, therefore, contaminated with bias and error: this is *God's own truth*, i.e., Truth with a capital *T*, divine truth otherwise inaccessible to women and men. Given these assumptions, the authoritarian principle of traditional Christian theology was quite reasonable; to proceed in theological work on any other basis than the authority of the Bible and tradition would have been absurd. Theology was thus quite properly understood as the exposition and intepretation of Christian doctrine, as found in the Bible and in subsequent Christian writers.

I do not think it is justifiable any longer to do Christian theology in this way. My reasons for this claim are worked out in my little book called *An Essay on Theological Method*,[1] and I shall not repeat them here. But it is not difficult to state briefly why this largely authoritarian approach is no longer tenable: it rests on a set of circular presuppositions that, once they are clearly seen, can no longer be accepted. Traditional theological work presupposes that we already know, even before we begin our theological investigations: (a) who or what God is, (b) that God is self-revealing and trustworthy (i.e., a being to which personal attributes can properly be ascribed), (c) that God has revealed Godself in the Bible and especially through Jesus Christ, and (d) that the proper method of interpretation of the Bible and tradition, enabling us to apprehend without serious error or distortion the divine revelation in them, is available to us. It is not difficult to see that each of these presuppositions of traditional theology is itself clearly a theological *issue*, i.e. it is not something that can be taken for granted but something which needs to be investigated and argued in the course of our theological work. We can see this immediately if we put these presuppositions into their correct form for examination, that is, as questions: (a) Are we justified in holding that we know at the outset of our work who or what God is? or is that something to be established in the course of theological inquiry? (b) Can we take it for granted that God is a personal being who reveals Godself to humanity, or is that a point to be investigated? (c) Is it justifiable, in the light of the great variety of religious claims and traditions of which we know today, simply to assume that God has fully and definitively deposited this self-revelation in the Bible or is that a claim to be explored? (d) Can we claim to know, without further investigation or argument, what is *the* correct and adequate way to intepret scripture and tradition?

None of these questions admits of easy answers; all require careful study and serious reflection. Yet very particular and definite answers to them all are presupposed when the authoritarian approach to theology, grounded on belief in a knowable and known divine revelation, is followed. Many of the most important theological questions with which we must concern ourselves today are thus begged by the authoritarian approach. It is not difficult to understand why such a *modus operandi* was followed by Christian believers of past generations who could take it for granted that they knew all these things; but for many contemporary people who have been shaped by the secularity and the religious pluralism of the modern world, these presuppositions have all become difficult

18

questions. What may have appeared to earlier Christians as certainties of faith have become for us problems. We can no longer, therefore, follow in our theological work a method that requires us to take for granted the ultimate authority and truth of tradition. We will have to proceed in some other way. But, if we cannot take for granted the fundamentals of the traditional Christian doctrines of God and of humanity in our attempt to come to some theological understanding of the nuclear crisis, how shall we proceed? What other conception of theology is available to us?

Let us look again at what theology has been in the past and how it has been done. The first thing we should note is a very obvious point, that theology is human work: theology is done by men and women for human purposes, and theological work is always assessed, therefore, by human standards invoked by ordinary human beings. The full significance of this fact has not often been taken into account by theologians. Since they took the basis of their work to be the very word or words of God, they held what they received from tradition in such reverence that it seemed inappropriate to criticize it radically or to reconstruct it in terms of their own best understanding or insights. This sort of attitude, however, is no longer justifiable. We are aware today that religious practices, institutions and beliefs have appeared in great variety in the course of history; and it seems evident that all such expressions have been much more the product of the creativity of the human spirit, attempting to find its way in the face of ever new problems and crises arising in life, than had traditionally been supposed. This is just as true of theology – of reflection on the language and ideas of faith – as of any other aspect of religious life or praxis. Theology also serves human purposes and needs, and it should be judged in terms of the adequacy with which it is fulfilling the objectives we humans set for it. 'The sabbath was made for man', Jesus said, 'not man for the sabbath' (Mark 2:27). That is, all religious institutions, practices, and ideas – including the idea of God – were made to serve human needs and to further our humanisation (what has traditionally been called our 'salvation'); humanity was not made for the sake of religious customs and ideas. In view of this it is really not surprising that, along with their reverence toward tradition, religious writers, prophets and theologians also have often been critical of the way it was understood and interpreted, and have called, in light of their own insights and understandings, for new conceptions in response to new perceived needs.

Theology has never, then, been simply the translation and handing on of tradition. As any study of the history of theological

19

ideas will show, whether we look at the supposedly authoritative biblical period or the elaborate subsequent developments of Christian history, it has always been a newly creative imaginative work of the theologian as well. Theologians (as well as others engaged in religious reflection) have examined and re-examined received ideas of God, criticizing them in light of the functions they were performing in human life and reconstructing them so they would serve more adequately as vehicles of humanisation; and it is important that we acknowledge the full significance of this fact in our attempt to define what theology can be and should be today. Theology is not merely a rehearsal and translation of tradition; it is (and always has been) a creative activity of the human imagination seeking to provide more adequate orientation for human life.

This reconsideration of the nature and function of theology brings us into a position from which we can see in a fresh way its task in the contemporary nuclear crisis. Theologians should not simply analyse the new situation in which we find ourselves in light of the basic claims of Christian faith, hoping to find some way to 'apply' traditional Christian insights to our problems: an approach of that sort assumes too easily that theology must do its work from within definitions and limits already laid down within tradition, that the fundamental conceptions with which it works are already given and nothing truly new and creative is to be expected. Such a view presupposes that the future is essentially closed, that it has already been encompassed and overcome by what has been given in the past and is made available in tradition. In effect it involves a denial that anything truly new and revolutionary can or will happen in the further unfolding of history. As we noted in the first chapter, a theology of this sort is not equipped to come to terms with the unanticipated situation in which we now find ourselves by virtue of the modern development of nuclear power. In contrast, however, if we understand theology to be the human spirit's creative and imaginative activity as it seeks orientation for itself in face of new historical contingencies and problems, the novelty of our situation presents itself as a challenge to be addressed rather than an embarrassment to be denied, overlooked or ignored.

How can Christian theology help to provide orientation and guidance in face of the nuclear threat which confronts all humankind? Religious reflection always works with the great symbols which have provided a particular historical community or civilisation with meaning and significance, as that community attempted to understand life and give it some order in institutions, customs and practices. In the case of the Christian world-view, two symbols above all have been fundamental and defining: *God*, and *Christ*. These have provided resources of meaning in terms of which all human existence was understood and given its basic order and significance. The other terms of the Christian vocabulary – sin, salvation, church, sacraments, trinity, gospel, and the like – all served to elaborate and articulate and spin out the full web of insights and connections made available by these grounding symbols of the Christian perspective. It should not be thought, of course, that the traffic here was only in one direction: that God and Christ were inexhaustible symbolic fountains pouring meaning into all the other concepts and symbols which structured the common life, thus providing existence with its significance. On the contrary, the creation and employment of terms like 'sin' and 'faith' and 'son of God' and 'trinity' each made their own contribution to the understanding of life and its possibilities and problems as grasped within the Christian perspective; they thus complexified and deepened and transformed in various ways the meanings which God and Christ came to have within the devotion and lives of women and men. Though these latter two symbols continued to ground the Christian web of meaning as the most basic points of reference in terms of which all else was understood, the meanings which they carried developed and deepened, as the other images and terms employed by Christians were increasingly elaborated, and as new life situations and problems made new demands. It is not surprising, therefore, that although the ultimate loyalty and commitment of virtually all Christians is directed toward God and Christ, they understand what this means in very diverse – even contradictory – ways, depending on the particular concrete content these and other Christian symbols have come to have for them.

A contemporary Christian theology conceived as imaginative construction (as I am proposing here) will continue to work with these two fundamental symbols, 'God' and 'Christ': it is these that give such reflection its distinctive character as *theology* (i.e., words or thinking about God) and as *Christ*ian. Christian theology is the attempt to think through and elaborate a perspective on life and the world which is illuminated by and oriented in terms of the resources of meaning made available to us in and through these grounding symbols. As such, it draws heavily, of course, on what these symbols have meant in the past, and it therefore needs to be well informed by the diverse traditions which have grown up in Christian history and by the theological definitions and elaborations

21

which have been worked out in those traditions. But these previous attempts to explore and define the Christian symbolic resources should not be regarded as binding or otherwise fundamentally limiting the theologian's work. To give past formulations and conceptions that sort of normative status for the present and the future would be idolatrous: we must ourselves take full responsibility for our definitions, our interpretations and our conclusions; and this may well lead us – as we face up to the radical novelty of the historical situation which we today confront – toward understandings and interpretations of our two fundamental symbols, God and Christ, which depart in important ways from dominant traditional views. Justification for any such new formulations, of course, can be given only as we proceed to the actual task of analysis, criticism and reconstruction of these symbols in light of the contingencies of contemporary life.

Let me now sum up and state systematically this conception of Christian theology as imaginative construction by presenting it in the form of three theses.

Thesis I

The proper business of Christian theology is the analysis, criticism, and reconstruction of the two grounding symbols of Christian faith, *God* and *Christ*.

Elucidation: This thesis has a number of implications which should be made explicit; above all, it rules out certain traditional ways of understanding the theological enterprise. In the first place, this thesis means that theology is not to be understood as primarily or chiefly exposition or interpretation of the several creeds of the church, or of the ideas of the Bible. Doubtless both the Bible and the creeds are relevant and important for understanding the image/concepts of God and Christ and for judging what are proper, and what improper, uses or formulations of these symbols; but it is their utility for getting at the notions of God and Christ that gives the Bible and the creeds their importance, not the other way around. God and Christ are the objects of our interest and concern here, and the Bible and the creeds are secondary to and derivative from that primary focus.

Other sorts of claims that are sometimes made about theology are similarly affected by our first thesis. It is often held, for instance, that Christian theology is primarily the exposition of Christian doctrines or dogmas, as though these doctrines and dogmas were givens which the theologian must accept, and which he or she is then called upon to explain or interpret. But according to our thesis this is once again the wrong way around. The only givens (and these are, as we shall see, very peculiar 'givens') with which the theologian works are the image/concepts of God and Christ as these have developed in history: all doctrines and dogmas are attempts to express and interpret the meanings of these symbols, and they have their significance in the degree to which they are successful in doing that.

It is sometimes said that theology is primarily anthropology, an interpretation of the nature of the human, and that therefore the first task in theology is to develop a conception of human existence. This is a more complex claim. Though we certainly cannot attain understanding of the meanings and uses of our two fundamental symbols without simultaneously working out a conception of certain features of human existence, and though different interpretations of the human condition, and different views of human nature, will have diverse implications for what or who we understand God or Christ to be, the distinctive task of Christian theology – that which distinguishes it from other disciplines – is not working out an understanding of humanity; it is, rather, to seek to understand and interpret (a) that supreme focus for human service and devotion, God, and (b) that historical complex of images and metaphors which makes the Christian conception of God and of humanity concrete and definite, namely Christ. A theological understanding of humanity must ultimately be dependent upon and in some respects derivative from what we conclude about God and Christ.

In the view I am presenting here all theology – Christian and other – is understood to be primarily a work of the imagination. This point can be grasped from two sides. On the one hand, by examining more closely what the image/concept of God has meant – how it has been understood, how it has functioned in human life from ancient Israel to the present, how the interpretations and the historical memories of Jesus of Nazareth have become connected with and integrated into it – we are enabled to see that the only human faculty that could have put together the notion of God, and which can continue to hold it before consciousness, is the imagination. On the other hand, if we remind ourselves that one of the most important functions of the imagination is to provide human existence with pictures of the world – of the context within which human life is lived and within which human existence, therefore, must be understood – we can see that all Christian God-talk, and everything associated with it (prayer, worship, meditation, repentance, obedience), belongs to a specific world-view, a specific interpretation of

23

human existence, created by the imagination in one particular historical stream of human culture to provide orientation in life for those living in that culture. In other cultural streams the imagination has produced other great world-pictures, and life lived in those settings has become oriented in other ways. The image/concepts of God and of Christ, and of human existence apprehended as 'under God' or 'in Christ', belong, thus, to one of many different frameworks of orientation for human life which the imagination has created in the course of history.

I wish now to elaborate further these two points with the help of my other two theses. First, a brief consideration of certain peculiarities of the image/concept 'God', which, I have suggested, it is theology's proper business – whether Christian, Jewish, Muslim, humanistic or other – to analyse and explicate. Then finally, a thesis about theology itself as an imaginative constructive activity.

Thesis II

The image/concept of God, a human construct like all other concepts and images, is, and always has been, built out of certain metaphors or images or models drawn from ordinary experience or history and then extrapolated or developed in such a way that it can serve as the ultimate point of reference for grasping and understanding all of experience, life, and the world.

Elucidation: There are two points being made in this second thesis. The first is that by *God* we mean to be indicating what may be called our 'ultimate point of reference', that in terms of which everything else is to be understood, that beyond which we cannot move in imagination, thought, or devotion. Traditional characterisations of God as well as more recent notions often make just this point. To refer to God as the 'creator of all things visible and invisible', for example, is to say that everything that exists has its source in God's activity and can be rightly understood only in relation to God's purposes for it. To think of God as 'lord' of history and of nature is to understand that everything which happens has its ultimate explanation in God's intention and action, that God's sovereign will lies behind the entire movement of nature and history, and that the real meaning of that movement, therefore, cannot be grasped without reference to what God is doing. To speak of God as 'the Alpha and the Omega' is explicitly to state that God defines or circumscribes everything else, and there is no way to get beyond God to something more ultimate or more significant. Referring to God as

24

the 'whence' of our sense of utter dependence (Schleiermacher), as Absolute Spirit (Hegel) or the Ground of Being (Tillich), is to make similar points from within somewhat different metaphysical commitments. By 'God', then, we mean the ultimate point of reference for all understanding of anything; by 'God' we mean the ultimate object of devotion for human life.

It is precisely this ultimacy, however interpreted mythically or metaphysically, that distinguishes God from all idols, and it is only because of this ultimacy that God can be considered an appropriate object of worship, a reality to which self and community may properly give themselves in unlimited devotion. To give oneself in worship and devotion to anything less than 'the ultimate point of reference' – anything less than God – would be to fall into bondage to some finite reality, eventually destroying the self and making true human fulfilment (that is, salvation), impossible. By 'God', then, we mean that reality, of whatever sort it may be, which rescues us from the idolatrous enslavements into which we continually fall, and brings human life to its full realisation. But it is only in virtue of being the 'ultimate point of reference' that God can in this way be the saviour from all idols.

If God has this kind of ultimacy – if God is in this way beyond everything finite, not to be identified directly with any of the realities of our experience in the world – then God is absolutely unique, and cannot be directly grasped or understood through any of our ordinary concepts or images. This is the second point being made in Thesis II. At best, all of the concepts and images with which we seek to conceive God and to understand God are only analogies or metaphors, symbols or models, drawn from human experience and history; they are, therefore, never applicable literally. The concept of God is built up in our minds by playing off one metaphor against another, by criticising and qualifying *this* image through juxtaposing it with *that* concept, by carefully selecting finite models which will enable us to gain some sense of that behind and beyond everything finite, that which cannot be identified directly with anything finite. Our concept of God, thus – if it is the 'ultimate point of reference' we are attempting to conceive – will never be finished or fixed in some particular form or image; it will always escape our every definition. As that 'than which nothing greater can be conceived' (to use Anselm's formula), God is beyond our every finite conception.

Thesis II implies that the way in which God is conceived is heavily dependent on the models and metaphors we use. A God conceived in terms of the metaphor of creativity or constructive power, for example, will be of a very different sort from a God conceived in terms of violent destructiveness; a God conceived in images of loving kindness and merciful forgiveness will be quite different from one conceived as impersonal process or abstract unity; a God conceived as definitively revealed in Jesus Christ will have a definiteness and concreteness unlike that of one believed to be seen everywhere and in everything – and thus nowhere in particular. There are many diverse notions of God abroad; the concrete models and images employed in constructing them are what distinguishes each from the others. A central task of theology is to become aware of the various metaphors, images and models which have been and can be used for putting together this symbol, and to develop criteria for choosing among them; a theology which seeks to be specifically Christian needs to locate the distinctively Christian images and conceptions, and to ascertain what special significance, if any, they might have. In the last two chapters I shall take up some of these matters. I must move on now, however, to my last point, which I will state in the form of Thesis III.

Thesis III

All theology, in its attempt to analyse, criticise, and reconstruct the image/concept of God, is an expression of the continuing activity of the human imagination seeking to create a framework of interpretation which can provide overall orientation for human life; theology is, thus, essentially an activity of imaginative construction.

Elucidation: An overall framework of interpretation which gives meaning to existence is indispensable to humans. We cannot gain orientation in life and cannot act without some conception or vision of the context within which we are living and moving, and without some understanding of our own place and role within that context. Only because of the imagination's power to unify and organise and synthesise into one grand vision what comes to us in experience episodically and in fragments are we enabled to make such attempts to grasp and understand and interpret the *whole* within which human life falls. In the various separated geographical settings in which humans gradually created great civilisations, quite diverse conceptions of the world, and of the human place within the world, developed, as the imagination generated and followed increasingly different perspectives in the several great cultural and religious traditions.

Among the world-views created by the imagination to provide orientation for human life was the theistic perspective generated particularly in ancient Israel. Here political and personal metaphors were utilised as the fundamental building blocks in putting together a conception of the world and of the human. The ultimate reality behind all else was the creator-God, a 'king' who had brought the world into being and now ruled it as a 'kingdom'. The world was envisioned as ordered by God's sovereign will, ruling through earthly intermediaries (kings or prophets or priests) who knew what God wanted done and sought to carry it out. Within this picture human life was to be lived in response to, and under the love and care of, the just, merciful and almighty God, the fundamental Reality behind all other reality, relationship to whom gives life its only proper orientation and meaning.

The images and concepts with which Christian theology works go back to this early mythopoeic activity in which a world-picture was created portraying all of life as derived from and ordered to God, the divine creator and king. It was, thus, this early constructive activity of the human imagination which first produced the fundamental theological images and concepts. This original mythic vision was gradually developed and shaped – constructed and reconstructed – during the several centuries of prophetic criticism and insight in Israel, and (particularly for Christian faith) under the impact of the ministry and death of Jesus of Nazareth and of subsequent interpretations of his significance. As Greek culture was encountered by those living within this theistic world-view, their reflection became philosophically self-conscious and critical, attending increasingly to problems of conceptual analysis and systematic conceptual construction; but it continued to work with images and concepts and metaphors derived from its mythic origins.

Although the constructive work of the imagination has in this way always been constitutive of theological activity, until recently theologians have seldom understood this. They have largely regarded themselves as attempting to express in human words and concepts what the divine king had objectively and authoritatively revealed to the church or synagogue. The fact that their work was thoroughly imaginative and constructive in character was simply not recognised. With the aid of the contemporary theory of world-views and conceptual frameworks, however, and of contemporary theory of the imagination, we are enabled to gain a fuller understanding of the human function and the logical standing of our religious and theological language; it is now appropriate as I have suggested here, for us to reconceive the theological enterprise as explicitly and essentially imaginative construction. Theological work now, therefore, can be carried on as a fully critical and self-conscious

27

constructive activity, in a way that has never before been possible.

This conception of theology opens a way for us to take full account of the radical novelty of the historical situation into which the discovery and massive development of nuclear weaponry has brought humankind. Our theological work need not be constrained in any way by the limitations of earlier interpretations of Christian symbolism, which had not anticipated this terrifying growth of human powers of destructiveness. All such earlier articulations of the Christian symbols (including those found in scripture), we can now see, were produced in and through the imaginative activity of men and women of earlier generations, attempting to come to terms with the problems of their lives and their worlds. These are, of course, indispensable in providing insight into the meaning and depth of these symbols, but they are in no way binding on us. Though our world is in many ways continuous with that of those earlier generations, it also differs significantly, for example in the great expansion of human technological knowledge and power, of which the possibility of nuclear catastrophe is the supreme symbol. It is in this world that we live, and it is orientation in face of these frightening problems that we need. It should not surprise us, therefore, if we come to an appropriation and articulation of the central Christian symbols which is different in significant respects from those which have traditionally been regarded as authoritative and true by Christians; indeed, precisely this should be expected.

A supreme test, one might say, of the ultimate viability, and thus finally of the truth, of the Christian symbols – or of any other symbolic frame of orientation for human life, for that matter – is their capacity to provide insight and guidance in our situation today, a situation in which humankind has come up against its own limits in a most decisive and paradoxical way: through gaining the power utterly to obliterate itself. If these symbols can nurture the contemporary Christian imagination in such a way as to call forth genuine insight and understanding of our desperate situation, and if the Christian imagination is sufficiently free and creative in probing the depths of and reconceiving these symbols to enable them truly to illumine these nearly opaque features of our life today, then Christian faith will continue to offer significant 'salvation' (to use the traditional word) to contemporary women and men. In the final two chapters I shall make some suggestions regarding the sort of theological reconception of the symbols of God and Christ that seems to me now required.

Notes

[1](Chico, California: Scholars Press, 1975; rev. ed., 1979.) See also *The Theological Imagination: Constructing the Concept of God* (Philadelphia: Westminster Press, 1981), esp. chs. 1 and 10. For a thorough historical analysis and deconstruction of the authoritarian approach within which traditional theology worked, see Edward Farley, *Ecclesial Reflection* (Philadelphia: Fortress Press, 1982).

III
Towards the reconception
of God

New ways of thinking are desperately needed in our time. We can see this at many different points in the complex of cultural crises that confront us. We now realise, for example, as earlier generations apparently did not, that the earth has quite limited resources and if we do not move quickly toward conservation of energy, water, minerals, arable land and so forth, human life as we know it can no longer be sustained. We are poisoning ourselves in many ways, some known to us, many unknown: the atmosphere, especially surrounding our cities, has become polluted and is dangerous to breathe; fish can no longer live in many of our rivers and lakes; the food that we eat apparently contains cancer-causing agents; 'acid rain' falls on our forests and kills the trees. It is clear that we dare no longer think in terms simply of meeting our immediate short-range needs, whether as individuals or as societies; if we do not take account of the long-range consequences of our activities, the ecological crisis in which we now live will deepen beyond repair.

New thinking is also required politically. It is no longer possible or appropriate for nation-states to regard their most fundamental task to be the defence, protection and enhancement of the way of life of their people. That has always been the first duty of politics, and the doctrine of national sovereignty has been its modern expression. According to this conception national strength shows itself most fully in the capacity to destroy a threatening enemy, in this way protecting oneself. We are now in a situation, however, in which destruction of the enemy can no longer be the ultimate method of defence. We continue, nevertheless, to be engaged in a spiraling arms race; and the prospect of nuclear catastrophe has become the outstanding symbol of the possibility – even the likelihood – that with our enormous technological power we are in fact bringing human history to its close. It is obvious that, before it is too late, we must learn to develop a politics of reduction of tension – of peace-making and of interdependence – rather than of self-protection and national sovereignty, but no one knows how to make effective moves in that direction.

In all of this our western religious symbolism has been more a hindrance than a help. It has been partially responsible for our ecological blindness, and it too easily lends itself to the re-inforcement and legitimation of our parochial political objectives. In the struggle between the USSR and the Euro-American allies, for example, we are regularly told – and most of us at least half believe – that this is God's battle we are fighting, and we are justified, therefore, in doing whatever is required to protect ourselves and, if necessary, to destroy the enemy. A religious and cosmic sanction to legitimate our own policy objectives is readily at hand, and it is not infrequently invoked. This gives us strength and courage in the great battle because of our confidence in God's omnipotent power: God is ultimately in control in this world and will surely bring victory, no matter how demonic or powerful are the forces in opposition. So we can be assured that, regardless of what action we find ourselves forced to take, all will come out well. For 'we know', as Paul put it, 'that all things work together for good to them that love God, to them who are the called according to his purpose' (Rom. 8:28 KJ). Religious convictions of this sort have their origins in the Bible, and they have given courage and confidence to many generations of Christians and Jews who found themselves engaged in desperate struggles to maintain their way of life against the threat of powerful enemies. The power, faithfulness and majesty of God, if it can be invoked in support of one's cause, one's way of life, is among the strongest motivations known to humankind. Belief in it has been a principal – if not the principal – grounding for faith, at least the faith nourished by the Psalms.

> God is our refuge and strength,
>   a very present help in trouble.
> Therefore we will not fear though
>   the earth should change,
> though the mountains shake in the
>   heart of the sea . . .
> The nations rage, the kingdoms totter;
>   he utters his voice, the earth melts.
> The Lord of hosts is with us;
>   the God of Jacob is our refuge (Ps. 46:1–2, 6–7).

31

Whatever justification there may have been for such symbolism in the past, in face of the magnitude of technological power now in the hands of human beings, it has become too risky to use. Such symbolism has often nourished and authorised massive historical evils: western imperialism and colonialism, slavery, unrestricted exploitation of the earth's resources, racism and sexism, persecution of those thought of as heretics or infidels, even attempts at genocide. We have come to a turn in human affairs in which such 'misunderstandings' or 'mistakes' (as we may view them in hindsight) are no longer tolerable. We must critically examine our religious symbolism and attempt to reconstruct it in ways that will more likely assure, so far as we can see, that it will function to good effect in human affairs. If we are to continue to employ the symbol 'God' at all, it will have to be in a much more carefully restricted form than most Christians have thus far acknowledged.

How shall we proceed with this reconstruction? If we may no longer simply appeal to traditional – particularly biblical – images and concepts in developing our understanding of God, what moves should we make? In chapter II I sketched an understanding of theology as involving primarily an activity of imaginative construction rather than appeal to and interpretation of authoritative tradition. I would like to suggest now, if only briefly and in outline, what this might mean with respect to the symbol 'God'.

We begin with God rather than, say, Christ, because the term 'God' has always been taken to refer to the ultimate point of reference for Christian faith, that which is at the origin of all things, including Christ, who is understood to have come from God (John 8:42), and to which all things ultimately return. 'For from him and to him and through him are all things', as Paul put it (Rom. 11:36). God is thus the first principle or the ultimate reality for Christian faith, and all else must be understood in its relation to God.

Just because God is taken to have this kind of significance, it is important that, at the outset of our constructive theological work, we keep our notion as formal as possible. For it is the concrete metaphors and images, which in religious devotion and service are connected to this 'ultimate point of reference', that give it specific content and meaning and thus enable it to provide actual guidance and orientation in the decisions and actions of everyday life; these, therefore, we will need to select with care. For example, thinking of God as 'our father in heaven' or as 'lord of hosts' or 'king of kings' inculcates and calls forth a sense that the proper relation to God is one of subordination, of respect and obedience to a dominant male figure of great authority and power, one who has intentions and purposes which 'he' is carrying out, one who issues commands we are to obey, one whom to cross or attempt to thwart would be disastrous, but one who, nevertheless, loves and cares for us like a parent. The concrete stories in the Bible and elsewhere which depict God as a character acting in some particular way, or which purport to say something (as in the parables of Jesus) of what the 'kingdom of God is like', all contribute specific content and meaning to the symbol; and more abstract notions like holiness and glory, righteousness and wrath, omnipotence and omniscience, infinitude and absoluteness, also add special qualities and meanings to the understanding of God. It is not, then, some merely formal 'ultimate point of reference' on which the believer meditates and to which he or she prays: it is a particular concretely conceived God who acts in fairly distinct and definite ways and who requires particular attitudes and modes of life and action from devotees. Obviously if God is conceived, as all too often in the Christian tradition, as a dominating kingly being, who is working in the world in a domineering all-powerful fashion and who demands of worshippers that they 'subdue' the earth and all its creatures (Gen. 1:28) and that they destroy without remainder all their enemies and God's (*cf.* Deut. 25:19; 1 Sam. 15:1–33; Rev. 17–18, etc.), a very powerful motivation toward a disciplined and authoritarian pattern of life will be engendered in the minds and hearts of believers, and corresponding character structures, social institutions and styles of life will be shaped, as believers seek to respond obediently to the almighty God and king who is their ruler and lord. The particular metaphors, images, and concepts, thus, by means of which we fill out and give concreteness and content to the ultimate point of reference, will decisively determine how God is understood as well as the sort of human relationship to God that is fitting and right. For this reason, as we seek to construct an image/concept of God suitable for orienting contemporary human existence with its unique problems, we must choose our metaphors and images carefully. What sort of criteria can be invoked to guide such choices?

I think it can be argued that the conception of an ultimate point of reference for human existence and the world, as it is expressed in the Christian understanding of God, performs two indispensable functions for human life, what we may call a 'relativising' function and a 'humanising' function.[1] The notion of an *ultimate* point of reference is connected with and articulates a sense of the deep mystery in everything, an awareness that nothing in our world has its reality and meaning simply in itself. In relation to the ultimate point of reference, everything in us and about us is relativised, is called into question; it is understood to have its true being and proper significance not in itself or through what we are and do and believe and understand but only in its relationship to God. The mythic notions of God as creator, as sovereign lord of life and history, as judge of all the earth, were often used in the tradition to express this relativising motif. To speak of God as the supreme relativiser, thus, is to refer in an abstract way to what may be perceived religiously as the mystery before whom we can only bow in awe and fear.

But in western religious traditions God has never been apprehended simply as awe-inspiring or terrifying: God has also been seen as the giver of all good gifts, including life and health and well-being; God has been worshipped as the saviour of humankind, the one who could and does bring human life to salvation and fulfilment. Along with the relativising dimension to the symbol 'God', there is also, thus, a profoundly humanising dimension: God is seen as ultimately a *humane* being, a 'father' (to use the symbolism of the tradition) who loves and cares for 'his' children, who grieves over their failures and their distresses and who willingly sacrifices everything – even 'his only son' – for their salvation and well-being.

It is the special 'genius' of the image/concept 'God', as I have suggested elsewhere, that it unites the relativising motif and the humanising motif and holds them together in one religious symbol.

> Thus that which serves to call into question everything we do and are and experience is at the same time apprehended as ultimately humane and beneficent, that which fulfils and completes our humanity; and that in which we can put our full confidence and trust and to which we can properly give ourselves in devotion is also that which requires a continuous criticism of ourselves, our values and ideas, our activities and customs and institutions.[2]

In our attempt to formulate an understanding of God for today, our principal concern should be to construct a symbol which can function both thoroughly to relativise and thoroughly to humanise our contemporary existence, institutions and activities. The principal criteria, thus, in terms of which we will undertake our constructive work, are 'relativisation' and 'humanisation' – not, as has usually been the case in theology, images and concepts more or less directly extracted from the Bible and other authoritative traditions.

We men and women today, as the women and men of any other time and place, experience ourselves as in many ways restricted, limited, relativised; and we also, all of us, receive our lives and our humanity as a gift from beyond ourselves. We know ourselves to be nourished and sustained and granted such well-being and human fulfilment as comes our way – i.e., we know ourselves to be humanised – by life-giving powers which we have not made and by circumstances largely out of our control. In many respects, therefore, we still experience our human existence as both relativised and humanised by forces and powers impinging from beyond us, from the context or matrix which has given birth to human life and which continues to sustain and transform it. It is through reflection on this contemporary experience and understanding of our relativisation and humanisation, and on that which unifies and holds these together in one, that we will begin to discern the outlines of a contemporary conception of God, of that ultimate point of reference to which we today can freely and wholeheartedly give ourselves in devotion and work.

Let us begin with the souces and sustaining powers from whence we come. Human life today is generally understood to be an expression of, and to be continually sustained by, the great web of life which has gradually emerged and evolved on planet earth. I cannot summarise here the long and complicated story of the evolution of life from primeval slime to innumerable higher forms, but it is not necessary to do so for it is a story well known to all. Human existence, as we understand it today, could never have come into being apart from this long process of differentiation and development. We humans must understand ourselves in the first place, therefore, as one strand in the very ancient and complex web of life, a strand, moreover, which would not exist apart from this context which has brought it forth and which continues to sustain it at every point.

However, these physical, chemical and biological conditions and developments were not all that was necessary to produce human existence as we know it. Once an animal had evolved with a sufficiently complex nervous system to sustain linguistic and other symbolic activity, thus making possible primitive consciousness, memory and imagination, a long and complicated *historical* development was required before anything that we would recognise as a truly human mode of existence could appear on earth. As increasingly complex forms of language developed over hundreds of generations, and experience, memory and imagination all became highly differentiated, humans began to experience their lives as transpiring within a wide context of memories and stories of the past as well as imagined possibilities and hopes for the future. Human creativity was born, together with intention and action, as humans found they could themselves actualise some of these possibilities

35

and hopes. Thus, human existence gradually developed qualities and capacities not found in any other form of life.

This all occurred, as I have suggested, not in a moment but over hundreds of generations. And it did not occur simply as a process of mental development. Increasing physical dexterity, upright posture, the development of the opposed thumb, and other changes making possible the invention and practice of new physical skills were occurring at the same time; and an increasingly complex brain and nervous system made it possible to coordinate these physical changes with a rapidly growing symbolic capacity. Humans invented simple, and then more complex, tools to facilitate their hunting for food and their protection of themselves against dangerous animals or against other tribes. They mastered the use of fire, and they learned how to make simple skin clothes, so they were able to move into colder climates and survive. As human life gradually became diversified with the development of new skills and activities, human societies became increasingly differentiated, since it was not possible for everyone to develop expertise in every area. So some became warriors and others gardeners, some hunters and others weavers, and some became chiefs – that is, those who coordinated and maintained and protected the orderly practice and interrelations of all these specialisations, so they would serve the well-being of the whole community.

Increasing specialisation made possible a high development of particular skills and crafts, and this in turn transformed human life in decisive ways, producing further new dimensions of experience and activity. The fine arts, politics, religious meditation and reflection on the meaning of life, all began to appear, later to be followed by philosophy, mathematics and the sciences. Thus, in the patterns played out in human activities, in the quantity and the quality of what men and women perceived to be needs that must be met, in the interests that increasingly occupied their attention and time, human life moved further and further from its animal origins. Though founded on and indissolubly interconnected with its biological foundations, it had become decisively historical and cultural in all its distinctive characteristics.

If we today are to speak of how we humans are created and sustained, it must be in terms of biological evolution and the eco-system, on the one hand, and the long process of human history and the diverse socio-cultural systems which it has produced, on the other. It is those complex conditions and developments that, so far as we can see, have made human life possible, and it is the continued working of these which presently sustain it. It is these conditions and developments that have both humanised and relativised us, and it is in connection with them, therefore, and the metaphors and images that they make available to us, that we today must come to understand and speak of God – if we are to speak of God at all in ways connected with our contemporary experience and knowledge.

The question might be raised at this point, if such a thoroughly naturalistic and historicistic account of human existence is accepted, why bother ourselves with attempting to speak of God? Is not the point of God-talk precisely to make a claim that it is a super-natural and super-historical reality which is the ultimate source and norm for human life? Is not the word 'God' a *name*, a name for that primordial reality beyond and outside of nature and history, and their common source, 'the creator of heaven and earth'? Certainly from the point of view of traditional usage, such questions are justified: God has usually (though by no means always) been thought of as a particular entity or being somehow beyond the finite order, and its source and ground. But we must remember now our methodological resolve: we will not take over, or regard as authoritative, traditional views simply because they are traditional; all of these without exception represent the imaginative constructions of earlier generations, and, however, instructive they may be for us, we have determined to do our own constructive theological work. The theologically significant function of the symbol 'God', we noted, is not that it names an entity or being which we might otherwise ignore or overlook, but rather that it focuses our consciousness and attention on that which humanises and relativises us. The proper criterion for our talk about God, we decided therefore, is not the postulation of some being or reality beyond the world but rather concern with the relativising and humanising activity going on within the world. Devotion to God and service to God are devotion and service to that which truly gives us our humanity and such fulfilment as may come our way, as well as limits and restricts and judges us when we overreach ourselves or seek that which can only harm or destroy us.

Let us return, then, to our attempt to understand the symbol 'God' in ecological terms, i.e., in connection with the biological and historical origins and grounding of human life. The boundary line between the historical and the biological – between that produced through human creativity and artifice, and that which is simply given – is not a sharp or clear one, and it would be a mistake to make too much of it. From their first appearance humans have been engaged in modifying the so-called givens of nature; and in thus creating the world of culture, which is now the immediate context of human life everywhere, they have produced an environment more hospitable to human existence as we know it. We have warm houses in winter and many have air-conditioning in the summer; we have hospitals to treat our diseases and mechanised agriculture to provide us with an enormous quantity and variety of foodstuffs; we are able to communicate instantaneously with any part of the globe, and we can fly to its most distant points in a matter of hours; we have literally transformed to the face of the earth – as can easily be seen by anyone approaching one of our great cities by air, or, for that matter, simply by walking down a city street. Moreover, we are rapidly approaching the time when we will be able intentionally to alter the genetic basis of human life, thus changing the actual physiological constitution of future generations; and it is no longer just a wild dream to imagine human beings leaving earth forever to make some other place in the universe their permanent home. The physical, chemical and biological conditions of human life are thus all malleable in many ways, and it would be a mistake to regard them as unalterable 'givens' which we must simply accept. One of the differences between the modern outlook on life and all ancient or classical viewpoints is this awareness that we are not simply at the disposal of mysterious cosmic powers that impinge upon us unilaterally from beyond – whether these are understood as fate or karma or the will of God – but that many, perhaps all, of the conditions which affect our existence and well-being are subject in certain respects to human modification and adjustment.

This picture of human life in its cosmic context differs sharply from the traditional theological portrait of humanity related to God. Two points in particular should be noted, both deriving from the fundamental complex of metaphors – the image/concept of the divine father-lord-creator – out of which the traditional conception of God was constructed. (a) In the traditional view, all that happened in the universe, from its creation until its end, was in its most significant respects the consequence of the sovereign will and action of God; God had set down the basic lines along which the history of the world would unfold, and God, as its omnipotent creator and lord, was sufficiently powerful and sufficiently constant in purpose to assure that cosmic and human history would reach their intended goals. (b) God's purposes for all of creation, and particularly for humankind, are beneficent and loving; God is a merciful parent, who rules the universe with perfect justice and love, and who desires nothing more than the ultimate well-being and fulfilment of each creature. The over-arching context of human life, thus, the purposive activity of the loving creator God, of which believers were assured in faith, gave a kind of security and confidence and hope that every conceivable evil which one might face in this life would be overcome. As the wonderful old Negro spiritual so movingly put it, 'He's got the whole wide world in his hands'.

The fundamental structure of this picture of human existence and its context is dualistic and asymmetrical. The omnipotent power and love of the divine creator-king determines absolutely and irrevocably the ultimate course and outcome of cosmic and human history: it is this which gives faith the assurance out of which it lives. But the modern world-picture which we have been considering is not structured in this way by an asymmetrical dualism, with a divine intentionality from on high determining unilaterally the course of cosmic evolution and human history. On the contrary, it is a picture of a unified and interdependent order in which deliberate intentionality appears only toward the end of a long evolutionary process on earth, as self-conscious beings emerge and gradually begin to take charge of their lives.

Although it is certainly possible, if one chooses, to affirm an understanding of God still rooted fundamentally in the traditional mythic picture – and many Christians are prepared to do this – it is clear that the asymmetrical dualism which gives that picture its force cannot illuminate many features of our situation today. In some respects the tables suggested by the old dualistic mythology appear to have almost completely turned: the cosmic order which is the source and context of our lives and our well-being suddenly seems to have no way to protect itself from the onslaught with which we humans now threaten it. We have developed the capacity to destroy ourselves and possibly all life on earth; our human intentionality and technological power have become portentous of calamity. In this situation we must find a conception of God more in accord with the modern notion of a fundamentally unified ecological order – and the contemporary crisis which it makes intelligible – if 'God' is to continue to be a viable symbol for orienting human life; for these appear today to the the actual context and the central problem of human existence.

We might, then, attempt to think of God in terms defined largely by the natural processes of cosmic and biological evolution. This would result in a God largely mute: one who, though active and moving with creativity and vitality, was essentially devoid of the kind of intentionality and care which characterised the heavenly father of tradition. Such a God could certainly evoke a piety of profound awe and respect, and even, in its own way, of love and trust. But it is not a God who could provide much guidance with respect to the great crises we today face, crises which are largely historical in character not biological, crises of human motivation, policy, action and institutions.

It is important to note at this point that a God conceived in this narrowly naturalistic way does not do justice to all the forces and conditions that have actually created our human existence. As we observed a moment ago, biological evolution by itself did not bring forth humanity as we know it: a long *historical* process of human cultural creativity was also required before self-conscious and self-directing life could appear. In consequence, human existence has become shaped by the institutions and language, the customs and skills, which women and men themselves created, and human purposes and meaning have come to permeate every dimension of life. If we are to think of God as that reality which actually humanises us, as well as relativises us, these matters will have to be taken into account.

This fact, that human existence has, in part, created itself in the course of creating an unfolding history – or rather, in creating a whole array of unfolding histories – complicates enormously our attempt to construct a contemporary understanding of God, of that which grounds and can orient human life. The divine activity which has given us our human being must apparently be conceived now as inseparable from, and as working in and through, the activity of the human spirit itself, as it creatively produces the cultures which make human life human.

It is, of course, not the case that men and women have, by taking thought and deliberate action, directly created themselves. For the most part human institutions and customs, ways of thinking and modes of social organisation, values and ideals, though certainly produced through human creativity and action, were not the direct consequences of anyone's deliberate intention or planning. Consider some examples: Modern science has certainly been a human creation, but no individual or group at the time of its origins in the seventeenth century had any notion of the complex institutional structures, modes of education and discipline, moral and communal commitments, financial and physical resources, not to say ways of thinking and patterns of theoretical explanation, which constitute science today. Though innumerable decisions and actions were certainly involved in the gradual evolution of modern democratic parliamentary institutions, no one simply thought out this mode of political organisation and then directly produced it. Every building to be found in any modern city is the product of human planning and intention – every brick was laid as a deliberate human act – but no one simply decided modern London or New York or Tokyo would be a fine thing to build, worked out the plans, and then brought it into being. The English language – or Chinese, or Sanskrit – is certainly a human creation, but who could be said to have taken thought and decided deliberately to create it?

We must say, then, that although every element of culture appears to be a product of human creativity, none of the great structures of history and culture – social institutions, customs, languages, patterns of reflection and understanding, complexes of value and meaning – was anticipated in human prevision or was the product of deliberate human intention. There is a hidden creativity at work in the historico-cultural process, and it is this which has given us the basic social and cultural structures which have actually created and continue to sustain human existence, as well as those qualities of life which we most deeply cherish: the consequences of our decisions and actions always far outrun our most ambitious purposes and our wildest dreams. It is the creativity working in and through history that has made human life distinctively human, and it is only in hope of continuing positive effects of this creativity – this unpredictable grace at work in our decisions and actions – that we today can take up the heavy responsibilities thrust upon us by the prodigious growth of technology and symbolised so dramatically by our stockpiles of nuclear weapons.

Let us collect our thoughts. We are attempting to find a contemporary way to think of God, to conceive that reality which grounds our existence, and devotion to which can provide us with significant orientation as we face the frightening pass to which human history has today come. We have seen that human existence was produced by and has emerged from an enormously complex configuration of physical, biological and historical processes, and these continue to sustain and nourish us both in body and in spirit; they both relativise us and continue to humanise us. Looking back through this long history of contingency and coincidence, it seems surprising that self-consciously cultivated human life was ever born on earth at all. But here we are, the product of creative cosmic processes we are far from understanding. If human life is to go on, all of the factors – physical, biological, and historico-cultural – which make it possible must remain in place, each making its indispensable contribution.

Devotion to God in our religious heritage has meant attention and gratitude to our creator, to that reality which brought us into being

41

and which continues to sustain us. Devotion and service to God seemed both natural and important to our forebears: natural, as an expression of the wonder and awe evoked by the awareness of having received the gift of life; important, in that consciousness of and response to the creator's will was indispensable if human life was to reach its intended fulfilment. This piety was focused by a mythic conception of God as a quasi-person, a conception fashioned with the aid of anthropomorphic images of lordship, parenthood and the making of artefacts. In many respects, as we have noted, the paternalistic and authoritarian overtones of this mythic notion – often destructive in the past – have now become seriously misleading and dangerous. This does not mean, however, that devotion to and service of God – that is, devotion to and service of that reality which has brought us into being, which continues to sustain us, and which draws us onward toward a fuller and more profound humanity – is any the less natural or important than before. What it does mean is that we must now conceive God in terms appropriate to our modern understanding of ourselves and the world, just as those earlier generations conceived God in terms drawn from and appropriate to their understanding of human life and those powers with which it had to come to terms. God should today be conceived in terms of the complex of physical, biological and historico-cultural conditions which have made human existence possible, which continue to sustain it, and which may draw it out to a fuller humanity and humaneness. Devotion to a God conceived in terms other than these will not be devotion to *God*, that is, to that reality which has (to our best understanding) in fact created us, and a living connection with which is in fact needed if our lives are to be sustained and nourished. It will be, in short, devotion to an idol, a pretender to divinity, and as such will be debilitating and destructive, and may in the end be disastrous.

Though we understand ourselves to have been brought into being by a complex configuration of factors, powers and processes (physical, vital and historico-cultural), it is appropriate to symbolise and hold all this together in the single symbol or concept, *God*. The function of our symbols, especially nouns and names, is to gather together for us, and hold together, those patterns and unities – found in the infinite manifold of experience – to which we need regularly attend if life is to have an order and meaning within which we can live and act appropriately and fruitfully. Thus, concepts like house or tree or even sandpile enable us, for certain purposes important to us, to grasp as unified and single what is, from other points of view, complex and diverse. The symbol 'God', as no other

42

name or concept in our western languages, holds together in a unity that complex reality which grounds and sustains our human existence, which both relativises and humanises us – that of which above all else, thus, we must be aware, and that to which above all else we must attend, if in our conscious reflection and in our action we are to be properly oriented in life and in the world. Only such a symbol or concept, which holds all this together in one, can enable us to focus effectively our meditation and activity.

Were we unable to consider the ground of our human existence to be significantly unified and unifying in the way the symbol 'God' suggests, our awareness of the oneness and integrity of our individual selfhood, as well as of our solidarity as humanity, would not be well supported; and we could easily fall into destructive patterns of language and thought and action. Such patterns have appeared all too often in our tradition: for example, the tendency to divide human beings into parts (like 'soul' and 'body'), seeking our 'essential nature' in only one dimension of our being and sacrificing other dimensions to that one; or the classification of humanity into categories such as 'male' and 'female' or 'black' and 'white', supposing that what is of real importance is more fully realised in one of these groups, which is thus deemed superior, more fully or paradigmatically human. But it is clearly a mistake to reify matter, life and spirit, and the different genders and races, into distinct and independent realities in their own rights, instead of treating them as abstractions from that more fundamental unity which constitutes our existence as human. Similarly, it is important to conceive the ultimate source and ground of this our integrated existence not as some merely composite or accidental aggregation: it must itself be significantly unified. Our symbol 'God', more fully and powerfully than any other in the language, directs attention to this ultimate unity behind and working through all dimensions of human life.

The symbol 'God' suggests a reality, an ultimate tendency or power, which is working itself out in an evolutionary process that has produced not only myriads of living species but also at least one living form able to shape and transform itself, through a cumulating history, into spirit, i.e., into a being in some measure self-conscious and free, living in a symbolical or cultural world which it has itself created. The symbol 'God' enables us to hold this whole grand evolutionary-historical sweep together as the cosmic movement which has both given us our humanity and which continues to call us to a deeper humanisation – which, that is to say, both relativises us at every point even while it continues to humanise us – a movement which we must understand as best we can and within

43

which we must live as responsibly and creatively as possible, if human life is to go on.

There is not space here to sketch out what it might mean to grasp our world and our existence as in this way of and from and in God, but I must conclude with a word about its implications for a theological understanding of the nuclear crisis. We have become aware in recent decades that 'life' is not a quality or power possessed by individual organisms but is rather a pervasive web of complex interconnections of which individual organisms and, indeed, entire species, are expressions, and apart from which they could not exist; and we humans spreading over the earth have been, especially in the last centuries, rupturing and poisoning that web, and polluting the natural environment which sustains it. We have, that is to say, been living and acting 'against God'; and despite the continuing activity of God (that is, of the forces that make for life and well-being) to overcome the evil we are working in the web of life on earth, the damage we are producing is extensive and it could end ultimately in the serious debilitation, or even the destruction, of human existence and of many other species as well.

As a strictly biological event, such an occurrence would probably be no calamity: many species have appeared on earth, thrived for a time, and then become extinct. But more must be said than that. For in the course of time the cosmic and divine order has brought forth a mode of being, a dimension of itself, that transcends in a significant way even the luxuriant fecundity of life, namely history – the symbolical order, the realm of spirit – within which consciousness and meaning, self-conscious subjectivity and purposiveness and freedom have reality. We humans are the only creatures we know who are the living incarnations of that distinctive mode of being. In this respect we are 'the point farthest out', so to speak, of the cosmic evolutionary-historical process, the point at which that movement of creativity has brought forth self-conscious selves, with the power to take some measure of direct responsiblity for the further unfolding of that very creativity. God – this whole grand cosmic evolutionary movement – is giving birth, after many millennia, to finite freedom and self-consciousness in and through our human history, in *us*; and before our human eyes a new and glorious vista – a hope – is gradually, over many generations, coming into view: a vision of life and community characterised by freedom, love, justice, meaning and creativity. This new age (if and as it comes), celebrated mythically in our religious traditions as the coming of the kingdom of God, will be (as some of those traditions themselves understood) a significant fulfilment and enhancement, a realisation, of God's

44

own being. It is a realisation, of course, that will come about, so far as humans can know, only as and if genuine community and full human personhood are actualised here on earth. In this respect God's own being and destiny with respect to earth – that is, what cosmic evolution and history ultimately are to mean here on earth – is intimately tied up with the course of human history. Thus the central Christian claim that God has irrevocably bound Godself to humanity by becoming incarnate in contingent human history receives momentous new meaning. Our fate on earth has become God's.

Although we can and certainly should hope that the creativity working in history will bring forth possibilities we cannot now foresee or intend, a pathway through the innumerable potential disasters that lie before us, this is not something on which we may rely with easy confidence (in the manner suggested by the traditional imagery of a providential God). Rather, our fate today is very much in our own hands, and we must take full responsibility for it. Moreover, the disaster we may bring forth upon the earth will not be one of merely human consequence, the obliteration of our species, and thus of our hopes and dreams. It will be, rather, a disaster for all of life, for the long, slow painful evolution through which life has proceeded here on earth, finally reaching new dimensions of meaning and value with the appearance of love and truth and self-consciousness and freedom as human history has unfolded. It will be, in short, a disaster for God, an enormous set-back for which we humans in this generation will have been responsible. It is this kind of historical and cosmic moment, a moment not even imaginable before our time, which we today must confront with open eyes and within which we must find a way to act responsibly and creatively and redemptively.

I will not attempt to recount here all that must be included in such action. Obviously, a dramatic and full transformation – a *metanoia* – of our major social, political and economic institutions, of our ways of thinking and acting, of the very structures of our selves, is required. Devotion to God, loyalty to God – conceived along the lines I have sketched here, which brings this powerfully evocative ancient symbol into connection with and support of our contemporary awareness of the interdependence of all life, indeed all reality – cannot be contented with any sort of private pietism or parochial concern for particular traditions and communities. It demands reflection on and action to bring about a *metanoia* in human life as a whole, for God is here understood as that ecological reality behind and in and working through all of life and history, and the

45

service of God can consist thus only in universally oriented vision and work. Devotion to God should help to break our loyalties to the less inclusive wholes and the more parochial centres of value to which we so often idolatrously give them in our ideological and patriotic and religious commitments. In this way it can, perhaps, help to open our eyes to some of the factors producing our furious rush toward race-suicide, and can inspire us to bring it to a halt. Awareness of God still means today, as it always has, that at the most fundamental level 'we are not our own' (cf. 1 Cor. 6:19), and what we do with our lives has significance of cosmic dimensions; but it also means, in a way that has not been so clearly visible in the traditional mythic imagery which gave birth to the idea of God, that since we humans now have the power to destroy human life on earth completely, what we do can have disastrous consequences for the divine life itself. Devotion to God today means, thus, that we resolve to make ourselves fully accountable for the continuance of life on earth.

Notes

[1] For elaboration of this claim, see *An Essay on Theological Method* (Chico, California: Scholars Press, rev. ed., 1979), ch. 3, and *The Theological Imagination* (Philadelphia: Westminster Press, 1981), chs. 1 and 10.
[2] *An Essay on Theological Method*, p. 56.

IV

Towards the reconception of Christ and salvation

One of the most ferocious persecutions in the history of Christianity – scarcely known to most Europeans and Americans, because our knowledge of Christianity is so largely limited to western history – occurred in Japan in the seventeenth century. After Christianity was introduced into Japan in 1549 by Francis Xavier, increasing numbers of Roman Catholic missionaries arrived, and by the end of the century there were hundreds of thousands of converts. Colleges, seminaries and hospitals were established, and for a time the Christians enjoyed considerable favour at the royal court. Before very long, however, certain political leaders became suspicious that the Christians were undermining the whole social and political structure of Japan – as, in certain respects, they were – and sporadic persecutions began. An edict of expulsion was promulgated in 1614, and after that persecution both of foreigners and of Japanese converts was fierce, with torture of all sorts, crucifixions, burnings, drownings: there were thousands of martyrs.

This situation of terror, torture and martyrdom is the setting for a novel by the contemporary Japanese writer Shusaku Endo entitled *Silence*. It is the silence of God, in face of the sufferings and deaths of those who had become faithful Christian believers, to which the title refers. The principal protagonist of the novel, a Portuguese missionary by the name of Sebastian Rodrigues – modelled on an actual historical figure – cannot understand why God seems never to respond to what is happening. In all the torture and suffering there is no sign from on high; the cries and prayers from the faithful bring no word of consolation. Sebastian begins to wonder whether God cares at all. Like so many other Christians who have struggled with the problem of suffering and evil, Sebastian finds himself unable to make any sense, in the Christian terms which he had been taught, of what is going on all around him. Finally, when he is himself subjected to terrible tortures and God still remains silent – with no response to his cries and prayers, no divine encouragement to stand fast – he apostasises.

The form of his apostasy was a standard one in the Japanese persecution. Christians were asked to place their foot down firmly on the crucifix, thus trampling underfoot the Christ in whom they had believed. Sebastian had long steeled himself for the moment when he would be faced with this demand. Now, after a considerable period of imprisonment, punctuated by various kinds of torture both subtle and gross, the moment is at hand. Sebastian faces the simple piece of copper metal fixed to a dirty gray plank immediately in front of him. These words run through his mind:

> Lord, since long, long ago innumerable times I have thought of your face. Especially since coming to this country I have done so tens of times. When I was in hiding in the mountains of Tomogi; when I crossed over in the little ship; . . . when I lay in prison at night. . . . Whenever I prayed your face appeared before me; when I was alone I thought of your face imparting a blessing; when I was captured your face as it appeared when you carried your cross gave me life. This face is deeply ingrained in my soul – the most beautiful, the most precious thing in the world has been living in my heart. And now with this foot I am going to trample on it.
> . . . [Sebastian then grasps the board with the crucifix on it] bringing it close to his eyes. He would like to press to his own face that face trampled on by so many feet. With saddened glance he stares intently at the man in the center . . ., worn down and hollow with the constant trampling. A tear is about to fall from his eye . . .
> 'It is only a formality', [he is told]. 'What do formalities matter? . . . Only go through with the exterior form of trampling.'
> The priest raises his foot. In it he feels a dull, heavy pain. This is no mere formality. He will now trample on what he has believed most pure, on what is filled with the ideals and the dreams of man. How his foot aches! And then the Christ in bronze speaks to the priest: 'Trample! Trample! I more than anyone know of the pain in your foot. Trample! It was to be trampled on by men that I was born into this world. It was to share men's pain that I carried my cross.'[1]

From its very beginnings Christian faith has been characterised by a deep ambivalence symbolised by the cross of Jesus, on the one hand, and by Jesus' resurrection, on the other. The cross, standing as it does for Jesus' suffering, self-sacrifice, death, meant that for Christianity suffering would be seen as of central importance to human life, indeed as the very vehicle of human salvation. As Isaiah 53, which was appropriated early by Christians to interpret the meaning of Jesus' crucifixion, put it: '. . . he was wounded for our transgressions, he was bruised for our iniquities; upon him was the chastisement that made us whole, and with his stripes we are healed' (53:5). Enormous human suffering, then, even torture and murder, are not simply evil: they may become, vicariously, the instrument of the redemption and transformation of others. The powerful Christian incentives toward self-giving, toward service of the weak, the poor, the unfortunate, toward self-sacrifice for others' well-being, which have always been central to the Christian ethic, are all rooted in this motif – symbolised by the cross – of the value and meaning of suffering for others. And the characteristic heroic figures of Christian history have not been those who exercised the magnificence of worldly power, but those, like St Francis or John Woolman, whose lives showed forth the virtues of patience, humility, kindness and long-suffering; or those, like Albert Schweitzer or Martin Luther King or Mother Teresa, who gave up much, perhaps even their lives, in the service of others.

But Christian faith has not been simply a matter of self-giving, as exemplified especially in Jesus' crucifixion. There has also been a strong motif of triumphalism in Christianity, symbolised above all by the resurrection. Jesus' sacrifice was not for nothing: in the end he was exalted to the right hand of God. And the sacrifices and self-giving of the faithful in this world will not be for nothing either: in the end they will receive their heavenly reward, the gift of eternal life in God's everlasting kingdom. When this prospect of eternal blessedness is coupled (as it often has been) with the expectation that some sort of everlasting torment in hell will be the ultimate fate of those who go counter to Christian teaching and practice, it clearly becomes a matter of simple self-interest to follow the Christian way in this world; for whatever cost or unhappiness one experiences in this life will be amply recompensed in the next. Thus, what at first seemed to be a motif of absolute self-sacrifice for others in the Christian symbolism, turns out on closer inspection to be rather an expression of prudential self-interest – given the sort of cosmic order in which we live, an order ruled by a divine king and judge who will mete out eternal rewards and punishments at the end of life or the end of time.

This reading of the Christian symbolism of death and resurrection, though somewhat crass, is far from unwarranted: it is directly rooted in the early Christian proclamation of the meaning of Jesus' crucifixion and what was called his resurrection. Paul expresses the ambivalence well in a familiar passage in Philippians 2. After reminding us that Jesus, though 'in the form of God' took upon himself the 'form of a servant', and then humbled himself even further to suffer death on a cross (2:6–8), Paul proudly declares that just because of this self-giving and self-humbling 'God has highly exalted him', giving him a 'name which is above every name, [so] that at the name of Jesus every knee should bow, in heaven and on earth and under the earth, and every tongue confess that Jesus Christ is Lord, to the glory of God the Father' (2:9–11).

Such use of the symbolism of cross and resurrection by Christians not only drew the sting from the motif of absolute self-sacrifice by transforming it into a kind of ultimate prudence and self-aggrandizement; it also laid foundations for later Christian imperialism. Christians soon came to believe that Jesus was really the only one through whom God's grace and salvation were mediated to men and women: '. . . there is salvation in no one else', as Peter put it in a speech reported in Acts, 'for there is no other name under heaven given among men by which we must be saved' (4:12). The true way of salvation for all humanity, then, was known only to the followers of Jesus. As christological conceptions became increasingly exalted and absolutised and reified, as symbols and doctrines were developed which interpreted Jesus not simply as the messiah of God but as the unique son of God, the *Logos* of God, the second person of the divine trinity, they seemed to imply that the keys to all human fulfilment and salvation had been placed exclusively in the hands of the church (*cf.* Mt. 16:18–19). It is hardly surprising that with this sort of exalted self-interpretation the church could easily be corrupted into crusades against the infidels and inquisitorial tortures and executions of heretics, and that it would ultimately give its blessing to western imperialism, and to the exploitation and enslavement of non-Christian peoples and cultures around the globe. The central christological symbols that emerged in the primitive church have been used to authorise these evils, and Christian symbolism, therefore, must bear some responsibility for them.

We are not here, however, primarily to praise or blame, but rather to understand and to reconstruct. What went wrong with this symbolism, and why did it go wrong? Is it so archaic, on the one hand, and so easily corruptible, on the other, that it should no longer be used but should be discarded completely, as some humanists would urge? Or are there elements in it that may still have significant salvific and redemptive uses? If so, how do we identify them and lift them out of the overall structure of Christian symbols which has become in many respects questionable and destructive? It should be obvious that a further employment of the chauvinistic and imperialistic side of traditional Christian symbolism is not what is wanted and needed in our age of potential nuclear holocaust.

I want to point out now that the problematic character of certain Christian symbols, which we have just been noting, is not directly rooted in the story of Jesus itself, but rather in the symbolic frame within which and by means of which that story was interpreted. That is, it was the understanding of the ultimate context of human life in terms of the symbol of God as creator-lord-father – the mythic conception of God which we examined in the last lecture – that made possible, perhaps inevitable, the development of this triumphalistic christology, not the story of Jesus itself. If we reconceive God along the lines suggested in the last chapter, a thorough reconstruction of the understanding of Christ will also be required. I hope to be able to show in this chapter that it will be an understanding that bears in a significant way on the profound crisis to which the availability of nuclear power and massive nuclear armaments has brought human affairs.

In the Jewish thought that was the background and context of early Christian thinking, God was conceived largely in terms of quasi-personal images, and the world was a quasi-political order in and through which the divine creator-king was working out 'his' purposes through history; it was expected that history would eventually reach its consummation as those purposes were realised. Jesus came preaching that this end of history was now at hand, and Jesus' followers thought of him as the Messiah who would inaugurate the divine kingdom on earth. After his unexpected death, they came to believe that he would soon return with heavenly hosts to overthrow all the evil powers resisting the divine will and would establish a new age of perfect peace and happiness. But none of this occurred in the way expected; and in due course Christians came to think of Jesus, God's unique son, as enthroned at the right hand of God and ruling the world from on high, where the faithful, after death, would join him in his heavenly kingdom.

The point I want to make here is that this entire interpretation is a development of the inherited mythic imagery of the universe as a political order ruled from on high by a divine king. Within this overall picture, human life is understood in terms of loyalty, faithfulness and love for the king and the order he has established (or is establishing). In various ways fellowship between the king and his subjects on earth has become disrupted and corrupted, but through the sacrifice of the king's son, the divine order has been re-established and it is now possible once again to live in faithful communion with the lord of the universe. One need only enter into the community of those who acknowledge Jesus as Lord, accepting this overall picture of the world and the human place within it – that is, one need only become a faithful member of the church – to find salvation from the evils of a world gone astray and a new life in communion with Christ, and through Christ with God. The meaning of Jesus' ministry, suffering and death, then – the historical core of the christology which became dominant in the church – is to be found in its role as a part of this grand drama of the salvation of humankind, which the creator-king is bringing about from on high.

It is not difficult to see how and why those committed to this mythology could easily become chauvinistic and imperialistic champions of the divine king and his son Jesus Christ, willing to fight to the death their adversaries on earth. In this mythicising of the Jesus story, the plain import of the suffering and death of Jesus – as a manifestation of real weakness in this world and of an unwillingness to use the means and methods of compulsive power to achieve objectives, as an expression of the strength to sacrifice himself completely even to his enemies – was lost sight of, and the crucifixion was seen as but one phase of the powerful working of salvation by God from on high; it was a phase, moreover, soon to be superseded and replaced in the triumph of Jesus' resurrection, in and through which all the evil powers on earth and under the earth – including even physical death – would be decisively overcome by the divine omnipotence.

The Christian tradition presents us, thus, with a deeply ambiguous christology. On the one hand, there is the picture of Jesus giving himself to others in service and healing, preaching and teaching that men and women should love and respect even their enemies, should do good to those who curse them, should become servants of all; and finally coming to the climax of his ministry in the suffering and complete sacrifice of himself in crucifixion – a picture of one who, as Endo says in his story, understood himself as coming into the world to be trampled upon by his fellow humans and who expected similar self-giving from his followers. On the other hand, there is the picture of Jesus the Christ, sitting at the right hand of God the Father almighty and moving history with omnipotent power toward its divinely set consummation, a consummation which is to include glorification and heavenly reward for all the Christian faithful. With such sharply distinct – even contradictory – motifs bound together at the very heart of the church's christological symbolism, it is not difficult to understand why Christian history has spawned such diverse and inconsistent emphases and movements and institutional patterns, each attempting in its own way to hold together in a dialectical vision these tensions and contradictions.

It is not difficult to understand either – human nature being what it is – why in most Christian movements most of the time the triumphalistic motif, with its promise of heavenly (or even earthly) reward became the dominant one, the motif of service and self-sacrifice sometimes being almost lost to sight. With such ambiguous symbolism at the heart of Christrian faith, quite diverse interpretations could each be given a certain plausibility; and almost any kind of institutional structure, social practice or political programme could be provided with religious legitimation. The possibilities for corrupt and dehumanising uses of Christian symbols were always present, and often, unfortunately, found expression. Yet at the same time this highly tensive christological core to Christian faith was a seedbed nurturing deeper awareness of and appreciation for the dignity and meaning of human persons, instilling in many believers revulsion against slavery, injustice and other forms of inhumanity and inspiring creative movements toward more humane social institutions and practices.

It is no longer appropriate for us to carry on our christological reflection within a framework characterised by such massive ambiguities. In the first place, as I argued in chapter III the highly personalistic and political imagery out of which the traditional conception of God was constructed is no longer viable and should not serve as the principal basis for theological reflection today or for religious piety – and it is precisely this symbolism, as we have just seen, that was a major source of the destructive ambiguity in traditional christology. Second, as I suggested in chapter II, once we have understood that all our religious images and concepts are the products of human imaginative creativity, attempting to provide orientation for human life in the world, we will see that, although traditional concepts and images deserve our deep respect and our careful study, they should not be taken as permanently authoritative or binding. We must take up full responsibility for ourselves in these matters and not take over uncritically the reflective and imaginative work of our forebears. Third, as I argued in chapter I, we live now in a radically new historical period, a time when it has become possible for humans by their own power to bring history to an end. This is a period and a possibility never anticipated in our religious traditions and for which they do not provide us with clear guidance. It is necessary, therefore, for us to think through our religious symbolism afresh, in face of the horrific possibilities that confront us as we seek orientation in today's world.

How shall we proceeed? Our analysis thus far has suggested that the traditional christology was an amalgam in which the tragic story of Jesus' ministry and death was interpreted in terms of, and thus combined with, an overarching conception of God as creator-lord-father of humankind and the world. A contemporary christology, presumably, should similarly attempt to examine and appropriate the story of Jesus in the light of a contemporary understanding of God, on the one hand, and of the most profound problems facing human existence today, on the other. If that story, when so interpreted, provides significant insight and orientation into human life and today's problems, christology can and should continue to have a place in our theological reflection and our religious devotion; if not, we should allow it to fall away so that we can come to terms with the issues with which the world today confronts us.

Historians are agreed that we possess little reliable information about the man Jesus of Nazareth. He was apparently an itinerant preacher and healer in first-century Palestine who believed that the kingdom of God was beginning to break into human history, bringing it to its end; his own healings of suffering and sickness, and his forgiveness of sins, were dramatic signs of the kingdom's coming. In his teaching Jesus emphasised the importance both of love to God and love to one's neighbors, and he gave this double-sided love a very radical meaning: it requires, for instance, repeatedly forgiving the offences of others against us ('seventy times seven', he told Peter, according to Matthew 18:22), going out of our way to help suffering fellow humans (as the story of 'the good Samaritan' suggests, Luke 10:29–37), always turning 'the other cheek' and going 'the second mile' (Matt. 5:39, 41), and all of this not only with friends but even with enemies (Matt. 5:43–7). The life to which Jesus called his followers involved a reversal of ordinary standards, where power over others is reckoned as signifying one's importance and serving others is regarded as demeaning: 'whoever would be great among you must be your servant', he said, and 'whoever would be first among you must be slave of all' (Mark 10:43–4). This radicalisation of moral demands by Jesus, and reversing of ordinary standards of significance or greatness, was brought into sharp and unforgettable focus by the final events of his life: he refused to defend or protect himself against his enemies, accepting meekly their whips and curses and finally suffering a violent death at their hands. Since the cross epitomised so well all that Jesus did and taught and stood for, it very early became a major symbol for Christian faith, signifying this self-giving, suffering and ultimate self-sacrifice.

We do not need to concern ourselves here with questions about the historical reliability of this or that detail of the story, or questions about whether these episodes and teachings can be taken as representative of Jesus' attitudes and behaviour in other situations of his life of which we have no record. Whatever probabilities or possibilities the historians may uncover with regard to such matters, and however fascinating these may be in themselves, they are not germane to our central interest here which is: what sort of image of the man Jesus comes through the portraits found in the New Testament? what sort of person is portrayed there? what were his central concerns? how did he relate to those round about him? for what did he give his life? On these matters the picture which we have is consistent and sharp, even though this or that detail may be historically questionable. We are presented with the portrait of a man who freely and willingly made himself, in Bonhoeffer's phrase, a 'man for others'.

What are we to make of an image and a story like that? Can it be regarded as in some sense redemptive or salvific for today's world? In approaching these questions we must not make the mistake of defining our expectations for salvation, and of Jesus' role in salvation, in the terms provided by tradition. The conception of sin as primarily a kind of personal disobedience or violation of the divine will, and salvation as being rescued from that condition of alienation and guilt, is rooted almost completely in the mythic picture which presents God as a divine king and father, and our relationship to God as the interpersonal and political one of subjects and children. Similarly, the traditional notion that what is needed by women and men in their condition of alienation and disobedience is God's forgiveness, an act of divine love restoring them to communion with God, and that Jesus' sacrifice on the cross in some way makes this possible, is a direct expression of this same personal/political picture of human existence and its context. But, as we noted in chapter III, human life can no longer be understood in terms of such an overly simplistic kind of personalism. Today we must think of it as emerging out of a long and complex evolutionary and historical development which included creation of both the biological eco-system and a whole complex of socio-cultural systems capable of sustaining human existence. Moreover, the most profound human problem today is not estrangement from God, as understood in such highly personalistic terms, but rather the steady undermining of the conditions that make meaningful and fruitful human life possible, through our pollution and poisoning of the eco-system, on the one hand, and through social and political and economic arrangements that are oppressive and dehumanising, on the other. The disastrous consequences of these directions in which we are moving, as we have observed, find their apocalyptic symbol in the threat of nuclear holocaust.

A conception of salvation or redemption appropriate to today's world and today's human problems will have to be framed in very different terms and employ quite different images from the familiar traditional ones. The role of Jesus, also, will need to be understood differently. When human life and its context was conceived almost exclusively in terms of familial and political models, it was natural and easy to think of human salvation as accomplished through the activities of a particular individual person, Jesus the Christ, who mediated between the Father in heaven and the wayward children on earth. But in the biological and historico-cultural terms with which we now conceive human existence, no individual person can have this sort of absolute significance and cosmic efficacy for all others, for every individual is an expression of and interdependent with the complex ecological web of life and nature which gives them all birth and sustains them all. Even God, as we have seen, should not be understood any longer as one individual over against all others but rather as the unifying symbol of those powers and dimensions of the ecological and historical feedback network which create and sustain and work to further enhance all life. Within this picture of human life and the world the meaning of the symbol 'Christ' will have to be conceived rather differently than in traditional christologies.

Attempting to sketch a christology and an interpretation of Christian salvation for today's world in the short space that remains to me can only result in vast oversimplifications, but I shall try to give some indication of what I have in mind. The fundamental human problem which we face – and which, we could also say, God faces – is how to bring about a reordering of human life and institutions which will, first, enable us gradually to move away from the likelihood of utterly destroying ourselves, either through nuclear disaster or increasing poisoning of ourselves and our environment; and second, will make possible a more humane, healthy and fulfilling existence for all women and men. Our objective, in the words of a recent World Council of Churches document, must be a truly 'just, participatory and sustainable society'.[2] It is obvious there can be no simple or pat solutions for problems of this magnitude and complexity, and for this reason religions should no longer attempt to present simple or single answers to the problems of life, nor should they insist that one particular path or way must be followed by all. Different persons and societies have diverse needs; what is possible and appropriate and good in one situation and context may be

56

pointless or destructive in another. Any understanding of salvation, then, and of the meaning of Christ today, must beware of simple cliché formulas and abstract universal rules or principles supposedly applying to everyone. It must beware, also, of attempting to understand the religious dimension of life in separation or abstraction from the political, economic, cultural, biological and other dimensions of the ecological and historical network which sustains us.

The problem of salvation is the problem of finding a way to keep all these diverse complexly interdependent dimensions of life in harmonious and fruitful balance and development. It is not a matter, therefore, to be dealt with by pastors and priests and theologians alone, by those who are experts largely in religious practices and traditions. It requires also the combined expertise and efforts of psychologists and chemists, engineers and artists, politicians and farmers, educators, physicians, labourers and many others, each making his or her unique and indispensable contribution to the common good. Salvation should no longer be conceived as a singular process or activity, a unilateral action from on high coming down to earth and working primarily in and through the church. Rather, it comprises all the activities and processes within human affairs which are helping to overcome the violence and disruptions and alienations, the various forms of oppression and exploitation, and all the other historical and institutional momentums today promoting personal and social deterioration and disintegration. In short, wherever a spirit of creativity and liberation and healing, of reconciliation and reconstruction, is at work in the world, there is to be seen saving activity. To give ourselves over to such reconciling and healing and liberating work in human affairs is to participate in the salvific work of the divine spirit.

If salvation is interpreted in such a broad way as this, it may be asked, has it not lost all distinctively Christian meaning? What do such vaguely constructive processes and activities and institutions as are suggested here have to do with Jesus the Christ?

Questions of this sort arise from a standpoint still largely informed by the traditional mythic picture of the divine salvific activity as uniquely the work of one particular person. I shall not repeat here again the reasons for rejecting that framework. Instead let me remind you that the New Testament, along with its mythic identification of salvation with the work of the divine man Jesus, also presents a somewhat larger view in which salvation is interpreted in terms of the presence of certain common – or uncommon – human dispositions and activities; for example, following Paul's listing in Galatians 5, 'love, joy, peace, patience, kindness, goodness', and the like, attitudes and virtues, that is to say, which express the spirit of reconciliation and healing working within human affairs. Similarly the writer of 1 John goes so far as to identify God, the primordial creative reality, directly with love, the same love that is found in human self-giving (4:8, 16); and he makes the presence of such love the very criterion of the presence of God, who is otherwise unseen and unknown: 'No man has ever seen God [he declares]; if we love one another, God abides in us and his love is perfected in us . . . If any one says, 'I love God', and hates his brother, he is a liar; for he who does not love his brother whom he has seen, cannot love God whom he has not seen' (4:12, 20). Doubtless both Paul and John, in accord with their generally mythic understanding of these matters, thought of these dispositions and activities of reconciliation and love as in a special way the supernatural working of the divine spirit in the Christian community; but what they actually described were attitudes and virtues known and recognisable in the Hellenistic world generally, ones for which the Greek language had common names.

It was, of course, the picture and story of Jesus, particularly his march to the cross, that so powerfully impressed upon these writers, and on the other early Christians as well, the significance of this particular configuration of dispositions and attitudes; and Jesus became viewed as their paradigmatic exemplification. But the attitudes and dispositions themselves did not belong uniquely to Jesus or to the early Christians: they were a selection from among the human and humane possibilities of life in the Hellenistic world of that time. That which makes a mode of existence 'Christian', thus, is not some supernatural quality or group of qualities made available only through Jesus Christ; it is, rather, the valuation as *normative for human life* of qualities and potentialities which make for reconciliation and loving community – those potentialities and qualities paradigmatically epitomised in the story of Jesus. And salvation is the ordering of human life – including its institutions and customs and social practices, as well as its interpersonal dimensions – in accord with this vision of human existence. All movements toward reconciliation and healing and liberation, toward overcoming oppression and alienation and deterioration, are to be understood as the activity of the salvific divine spirit – the spirit of Christ – at work in the world.

It is interesting, and I think significant, that already in the earliest period of Christian history some saw quite clearly that salvation consisted essentially in a particular mode and quality of life, not in consciousness of some special connectedness with Jesus, and they made this point sharply and explicitly by putting it in the mouth of Jesus himself. In the parable of the last judgement reported in Matthew 25, those approved are not the ones who worried about their connection with Christ but instead those who spontaneously gave a cup of cold water to the thirsty, who clothed the naked and visited the sick and imprisoned. It is these latter who are said to be responding to Christ and expressing his spirit. 'Truly . . . as you did it to one of the least of these my brethren, you did it to me' (25:40). In another place Matthew reports Jesus as saying, 'Not every one who says to me, "Lord, Lord" shall enter the kingdom of heaven, but he who does the will of my Father who is in heaven' (7:21) – that is, those who are engaged in activities of actual reconciliation and healing, not those who are fastidious about identifying themselves with Christ or the church, are the ones through whom the divine salvific activity is at work.

One might ask, What religious point has a salvation of this sort? Why concern oneself with it at all? Why bother to be a Christian? Under the old mythic understanding of salvation the answer to such questions was simple and straightforward: here, and here alone, is to be found forgiveness of one's sins, peace with God, genuine fulfilment, eternal life. There were, thus, very powerful – if, perhaps, somewhat self-interested – incentives to believe. But what does the salvation I have been describing have to offer?

It must be acknowledged immediately that this understanding of salvation cannot appeal directly to motives of self-interest: neither a peaceful and contented life on earth, nor eternal bliss in heaven is its expected reward. On the contrary, radical self-giving in struggle with the worst evils of contemporary human life, culminating perhaps in complete self-sacrifice – crucifixion – is what is to be expected. The only reward promised here is the consciousness that one is expending one's life and energy to help liberate men and women from the evils which presently enslave them; one is seeking to help make future human life more humane and fulfilling than life today; one is giving up oneself for others. We are, after all, fundamentally social beings belonging to and constituting each other, not individual atomic egos living by and to ourselves alone; and our deepest human satisfaction, it can be maintained, comes, therefore, not in individualistic self-realisation but rather in contributing to the well-being of those in the midst of whom we have our lives, in helping to enhance the quality of life for others.

This claim that it is only in losing our lives that we are saved is of course very controversial and by no means universally accepted. It is, however, and always has been, central to the Christian vision, though the Christian tradition itself, as we have seen, has been deeply ambivalent about it. It is the motif in the Christian story which bears most obviously on our present historical situation and which points most clearly the direction humankind must increasingly move if we are not to destroy ourselves.

Human life to this point in history has organised itself as a multiplicity of centres – individuals, groups, nations – each of which understands itself as justified in pursuing its own objectives, in seeking to realise and perpetuate its own values and way of life, in defending itself against those who would destroy it. Self-realisation is the goal of each such centre; self-defence is its ultimate inalienable right. Religious traditions, idealised visions of many sorts, patriotic feelings, loyalty to those whom one loves – all these legitimate and encourage the struggles of each such centre to develop itself in its own terms and to protect itself from its enemies, both spiritual and physical. It is this whole pervasive pattern of human existence, divided up into many and various distinct spheres each of which is concerned primarily with its own interests, that has now become so dangerous that it must go. Life itself has a structure of interdependence, and unless human living and thinking and working can become increasingly oriented accordingly, and we learn to subordinate our particular interests and desires as individuals and communities, as religions and value traditions, as social classes and nation-states, to this wider loyalty to on-going life – both human and other – we shall certainly all perish. The Christian vision, then, focused on the portrait of that one who came into the world 'not to be served, but to serve, and to give his life as a ransom for many' (Mt. 20:28), assumes a new pertinence and significance in our time. Precisely this sort of giving up to and for others is now required of us all – individuals, communities, classes, institutions, religious traditions, nations. It is particularly required of those of us who live in the affluence of the so-called 'first world', and who have, therefore, so much which we can give up for others – if we are only willing to part with it.[3] The Christian vision, with its understanding that ultimately we are not our own – we come from and belong to God, that wider stream of self-giving creativity and life which has brought us into being and of which we are a part – and that we are called to live, therefore, in continuous self-giving to and for others, and in this alone will we find fulfilment, presents an orientation for human existence precisely appropriate to the most urgent demands of our time. The self-sacrificial Jesus is able to call us back to the foundations of our being because his act of self-giving is a paradigmatic image and symbol of something at the very heart of those foundations: the interdependence and self-giving which underlies and makes possible all creativity and life, the very structure or activity which Christians call God.

Let me, in conclusion, qualify these sweeping claims in two important respects. My use of Endo's dramatic story of Christ as the one to be trampled upon, and my invocation of the motif of self-sacrifice in the Christian vision, may suggest that I am advocating a kind of simplistic stance of humility and self-denial as the solution to all the world's problems – a position that has not infrequently found expression in Christian history, especially in admonitions to servants and slaves, poor people and women, to remember that their place in life is caring for the needs and desires of others. I do not want to be identified with any such position. Many of the concrete situations of injustice and inhumanity in today's world require the firmest possible resistance by those oppressed and the strongest possible insistence that the conditions under which they live be changed. Our christological paradigm provides no universal panacea for all the diverse conditions and situations of evil in human affairs, and neither Jesus' commandment to love our enemies nor the march of Jesus to the cross should be interpreted literalistically as defining the right pattern of action for every situation. To take such a position would be to absolutise one particular pattern or prescription inherited from the past as applicable and appropriate always and everywhere. But it is just such freezing or reifying of the insights of one moment in history into dogmatic truths supposed eternally valid, that I have been criticising here as a principal problem with traditional Christian reflection, and that my conception of theology as requiring fresh imaginative construction in each new age is intended to replace.

The Christian tradition does not provide us with concrete and particular answers to the concrete and particular problems we must face; to interpret it in that way is to make it into one more idol which will only deepen our difficulties. What the Christian tradition can give us is a vision of the overall character and shape which human life must assume if it is to find salvation or fulfilment – indeed, if it is to survive: an orientation (in both individuals and groups) of radical self-denial for the sake of wider communities, ultimately for the universal community that includes all beings (the 'kingdom of God'). And it can provide us with a dramatic and powerful image, in Jesus' crucifixion, of what is involved in this thorough 'trans-valuation' (Nietzsche) of all our ordinary values and ways of thinking, of our patterns of action and institutional arrangements. It presents us, thus, with symbols and images and values which can orient our lives today and can provide guidance for our actions and policies. But – with whatever help such orientation gives us – it is we ourselves who will have to find our way through the enormously complex and difficult tangles and thickets which humankind now faces, including the nuclear dilemma. Our problems today, as we have seen, lie across the whole range of economic, political, social, intellectual, moral and religious dimensions of life. They interpenetrate each other in very complicated ways, and there can be no simplistic solution for them. It will tax the imagination, creativity and devotion of all of us to address them successfully while there is still time.

I would like to say one final word about another kind of misunderstanding to which the reconception of Christ and salvation which I have presented may lend itself. Some may regard this interpretation as but one more chauvinistic or imperialistic attempt to show that Christianity is really the true religion to which all persons should be converted, all other religions being in varying degrees inappropriate or false. This is certainly not my intention or my claim, and I would like to remind you that in principle the understanding of theology as imaginative construction should undermine all such arrogance. What I have tried to do in this book is think in a fresh way about the symbols 'God' and 'Christ' in face of the potential nuclear catastrophe that confronts us all, hoping to find within them some light or guidance or orientation for the difficult and unknown path we must search out in today's world. In many of the forms it has taken historically, the Christian structure of symbols has serious limitations and drawbacks, and I have not hesitated to point out some of these. But there remain depths of meaning and profundity in the central Christian symbols, I am persuaded, which are worth our attention as we face one of the most frightening dilemmas with which history has confronted humankind.

This does not mean that other religious or secular visions do not also have much to offer. We are in a situation in which the future of humanity is at stake, and it behoves us to bring all the wisdom and devotion and insight accumulated through our long history to bear on our problems. Buddhists and Hindus, Jews and Moslems, Africans and Chinese, Marxists and Freudians, liberals and conservatives, ordinary folk and sophisticated intellectuals, will all, doubtless, have their contributions to make to our common task. None of us knows a sure way through our present moment in history: those dogmatists who think they do are the greatest danger to us all. We must, therefore, work together toward the common goal and the common good, drawing upon whatever resources – religious or secular, philosophical or poetic, mythic or scientific – are available to us, and offering them to each other as we grope toward an unknown future. It is in this spirit, hoping to make some small contribution to the task confronting us all, that I present these reflections on the reconstruction of Christian theology for a nuclear age.

Notes

[1](Tokyo, New York and San Francisco: Kodansha International Ltd. 1969), pp. 270–1. Published by Peter Owen Ltd in London and Taplinger Publishing Co. in New York, and used by permission.
[2]See *Faith, Science and the Future,* ed. Paul Abrecht (Philadelphia: Fortress Press, 1978).
[3]See Marie Augusta Neal, *A Socio-Theology of Letting Go* (New York: Paulist Press, 1977).

Index